QUALITY CARE
for
TOUGH KIDS

Studies

of the Maintenance of Subsidized Foster Placements in

The Casey Family Program

D0561613

James A. Walsh and Roberta A. Walsh

Child Welfare League of America
Washington, DC

Copyright © 1990 by the Child Welfare League of America, Inc.

All Rights Reserved. Neither this book nor any part may be reproduced or transmitted in any form or by any means, electronic or mechanical, including photocopying, microfilming, and recording, or by any information storage and retrieval system, without permission in writing from the publisher. For information on this or other CWLA publications, contact the CWLA Publications Department at the address below.

CHILD WELFARE LEAGUE OF AMERICA, INC.
440 First Street, NW, Suite 310, Washington, DC 20001-2085

CURRENT PRINTING (last digit)
10 9 8 7 6 5 4 3 2 1

Cover design by Kevin Erskine
Text design by Rose Jacobowitz

Printed in the United States of America

Library of Congress Cataloging-in-Publication Data

Walsh, James A., 1938–
    Quality care for tough kids : studies of the maintenance of
subsidized foster placements in the Casey Family Program / James A.
Walsh and Roberta A. Walsh.
        p.   cm.
    Includes bibliographical references.
    ISBN 0-87868-372-0 : $18.95
    1. Foster home care—United States—Case studies.   2. Foster
children—United States—Case studies.   3. Casey Family Program.
I. Walsh, Roberta A.   II. Title.
HV881.W35   1990
362.7'33'0973—dc20

90-35239
CIP

Contents

4   DESCRIPTIVE SUMMARY OF THE CHILDREN OF THE MONTANA DIVISION,   43

5   STUDY I   PREDICTION OF OUTCOMES,   53

Preface

The pages that follow describe three studies of the maintenance of subsidized foster placements in The Casey Family Program. The main thrust of the research was to discover factors that were associated with stable foster placements, and correlational methods were used extensively. Although a few relatively sophisticated procedures were employed, readers can proceed with confidence if they are familiar with the concepts of mean, standard deviation, and correlation coefficient.

Many of the potential predictors of placement maintenance that we investigated are psychodynamic in origin, but we have not stressed dynamic factors in the explanation of our results. We have abstained from such discussions not because we are uncomfortable with them, but because they frequently carry with them implications of cause and effect that our experimental design and methodology cannot support. For the same reason we have tried to keep to a minimum any statements about what caused what, except in a few sections where causal relationships seem inherent in the data. Our research is primarily correlational, and we have reminded the reader of its limitations in that respect.

The roots of much of our work are in the child welfare, foster care, and child development literatures. We have not cited those bodies of work in any systematic way; in fact, we have referenced primarily methodological books and papers that may be unfamiliar to some of our readers. Our purpose is not to avoid the task of scholarly documentation, but rather to avoid the implication that our results apply directly to foster care as it is practiced in the United States at the present time. The children of The Casey Family Program are not a random sample of those who are currently in need of foster care; they are instead selected from the consistent underachievers of that population. Nor is The Casey Family Program representative of the organizations providing foster care in contemporary American society. It is a richly subsidized organization of highly trained professionals working under quite favorable conditions. Thus, it may be the case that our results will be shown to be applicable only within the rather special environment currently enjoyed by The Casey Family Program. Should this be so, we hope that our efforts will at least serve to broaden the perspective of child welfare research to include more nontraditional approaches to care.

Throughout this book we speak of the "children" of The Casey Family Program. Some are indeed children, others are adolescents, some are young adults. "Children" is simply a convenient noun to describe all of the young people served by The Casey Family Program. The vignettes of Casey Family young people that are scattered through this book are based on real children and real families. Names and details have, of course, been changed to preserve their privacy.

The first study we describe had its beginnings in 1980, and the last was finished in 1985. During that time many people have been helpful. Vincent Matule, former director of the Montana Division of The Casey Family Program, was supportive, constructive, and inspirational in the initiation and conduct of this work. His staff, especially Darrell Glasscock, Lowell Luke, and Suzanne Larsen, were of tremendous help. Hildegarde Mauzerall, director of the Idaho Division, and her staff provided assistance and encouragement. Margaret Stuart of the social work faculty of Carroll College contributed materially to the substance of this research. Carl Erickson and Arthur Dodson, executive directors of The Casey Family Program during the period of these studies, and the Board of Trustees have been unfailing in their encouragement of our efforts. Finally, and far from least, Linda Richtmyer and Helen Utsond have typed and retyped endless revisions of this manuscript with patience, expertise, and good humor. Our thanks to all.

1

A Bit of History

Foster care has a long history. Accounts of cross-fostering the sons of the nobility date from at least the time of Alexander the Great. But large-scale, systematic placement of children in foster homes is a comparatively recent practice, and recognition of the need to assess placements and outcomes is probably only a few decades old.

For the past seven years we have studied placements and placement outcomes within a large private system of foster care, The Casey Family Program. We focused particularly on how to predict the maintenance of a foster placement when foster children have been matched with foster parents in what is intended to be a long-term, stable relationship. Using statistical prediction techniques, we built models of placement mainte-nance based on characteristics of the foster child, his or her biological family, and the foster family. We used two principal sources of data: archival material on the foster child and biological family, and caseworker ratings of characteristics of foster child and foster family.

With data from one division of The Casey Family Program we built a predictive model, which we then cross-validated in a second division. We investigated behavioral and other brief methods of assessing variables that turned out to be of predictive importance to determine whether they were practically and economically feasible to use. In a majority of cases they were, and the predictions based on the model were quite accurate compared to most contemporary work in social and behavioral science.

For the success of our predictive efforts, described in the following chapters, we credit the organization and structure of The Casey Family Program. Given its size and its status as the largest planned program of private long-term foster care in the United States, relatively little is known to either the general public or interested professionals about its history and operation. We will devote a few pages to remedying this situation, for The Casey Family Program has an unusually interesting history, tied as it is to the life and career of a pioneer of twentieth-century American industry, Jim Casey.

Casey's Beginnings

Casey was born in a Nevada mining town in 1888. His father, a prospector and small-time hotel keeper, moved the family to Seattle about 1890 to share in the boom Seattle was then enjoying. But Seattle's fortunes fluctuated with the country's economy, and the Casey family's fortunes followed suit.

Casey's father fell ill around the turn of the century, so at age 11 Jim left school and became a messenger boy for a department store at $2.50 a month to help support his parents, two younger brothers, and a younger sister.

By the time he was 19, Casey had started his own messenger service with a partner, Everett McCabe, but gave it up for a stint of prospecting in Nevada. When he returned to Seattle, he and Claude Ryan founded the American Messenger Service. The prospects of AMS, originally capitalized for $100 and operated from a 6- by 17-foot basement in a Seattle saloon, must have seemed limited to Ryan, because he sold Casey his company holdings in 1917.

In 1919 Casey renamed his operation United Parcel Service and began expanding it to major west coast cities. By 1930, United Parcel was serving customers from San Diego to Seattle, and Casey decided to try his luck in New York. There he quickly garnered several major customers with a combination of low rates, fast and reliable service, and shrewd advertising.

Casey was not, however, primarily a marketer. More interested in the mechanized and the human sides of his operations, he was an innovative designer of machinery to move packages faster and more safely and a motivator of the men and women who worked for him. Long before the Japanese, Casey had implemented participatory management and profit sharing for company employees.

Although he achieved extravagant success at a relatively early age, Casey lived simply. His personal life revolved around his mother, brothers, and sister. Long after his company had become preeminent in its field and his financial worth enormous, he focused on his work and especially on ways to motivate and maintain the highly productive UPS work force.

The Casey Family Program's Beginnings

From at least the mid-1950s, Casey and his brothers, George and Harry, and sister, Marguerite, had discussed how to use the funds placed in a foundation set up to honor their mother in such a way as to help needy children. Not long after George's death in 1957, Casey, Harry, and Marguerite, apparently regretting that they had not moved ahead with their plans while George was alive to see their results, decided to concentrate on a project for providing long-term care for especially disadvantaged children.

In his usual systematic way, Casey began to read in the New York Public Library about foster care and quickly came across some of the Child Welfare League of America's literature. He soon had a grasp of the way the foster care system functioned and began to look at its strengths and weaknesses and to consider ways to make it more effective.

In 1965, 77 years old and about to retire as UPS board chairman, Casey felt confident enough of his ideas to approach Joseph Reid, at that time head of the Child Welfare League of America. There is a story, perhaps apocryphal but with legendary status, that Casey appeared unannounced at Reid's office, got in to see him without introducing himself other than to say he was associated with UPS, and explained to Reid that CWLA was going about things in the wrong way. Instead of depending upon volunteer families to provide foster care for relatively short time periods, he told Reid, CWLA should search out strong families, make them aware of the challenges and rewards of providing foster care, and then pay them to provide the best and most supportive possible long-term environment for a foster child. And, he told Reid, the children for whom such care was most important were the unfortunates who could not return to their own families. Reid listened courteously to his visitor and promised to speak with him again when he had had a chance to think over his suggestions.

As soon as Casey left the office, Reid asked his secretary to find out what she could about the tall, lean man with the impressive manner. With one or two phone calls she identified Casey and clarified the dimensions of his accomplishment and wealth. Excited about the opportunity that seemed to be opening up, Reid spent several days considering Casey's ideas and their implications.

At their second meeting, Casey and Reid outlined a plan that leaned heavily on three assumptions. First, the foster children with the worst long-term prospects come from the poorest and most disorganized families, to which they could not realistically hope to return. A program for these consistent underachievers in the child welfare system could make a unique contribution. Second, for long-term success, a program needs a planned approach to meeting a child's needs over the span of his or her development. Third, the approach should combine what child welfare professionals know about foster children and what successful managers know about organization and motivation, particularly the role of financial incentives. Reid clearly supported the proposal, and Casey proceeded to construct the framework of his new organization.

Casey began his program in Seattle, a city he had known well for more than 70 years, and where he could draw upon the talents of friends and associates to form a board of trustees. As the nucleus of his board, in addition to his sister, Marguerite, he recruited John Riese, an attorney; A. V. Nelson, an accountant; Charles Rehm, a physician; George Fahey, a clothier and retailer; and Elwood Hall, a banker. The professional qualifications of these individuals mattered less to Casey than the integrity and sound judgment they had demonstrated over an association of many years.

The board began by seeking advice and support of local social service groups, especially those of the Catholic archdiocese. As a young man Casey had seen many examples of the dedicated work of those services, and as a member of a staunch and traditional Irish Catholic family he would have preferred to coordinate his efforts with those of the Catholic church. Bishop Gill was not encouraging, however, and the board eventually found itself working with United Way in doing a feasibility study of Casey's proposal.

With this foundation, Casey and his board began searching for an administrator—someone familiar with the child welfare system, interested in working in an innovative program, and qualified to build and lead such an organization. They chose Paul Christiansen, then chief probation officer of Snohomish County just north of Seattle, and hired him to begin operations on July 1, 1966.

Although Christiansen had to build this operation from the ground up, he had two major advantages that allowed him to move relatively quickly. His board was composed of extremely knowledgeable individuals with entrée to municipal, corporate, and social corridors of power. In addition, the vast financial resources of the Annie E. Casey Foundation, named after Casey's then recently deceased mother, were unstintingly brought to bear upon the fledgling organization's problems. The Casey

Family Program did not solve problems by simply throwing money at them, but it knew how to employ its fiscal resources to conserve and make the best use of its human ones.

With some valuable advice and support from United Way personnel, Christiansen began seeking out children, primarily disadvantaged ones with little or no prospect of returning to their own homes. He placed them in foster families selected as likely to provide stable, long-term placements. Building carefully but steadily, and always with an eye out for good families and high-quality professional staff members, Christiansen had 100 children in foster care by 1972.

That year brought several important changes in The Casey Family Program. Until then, the program operated one geographically compact organization centered on Seattle. Fewer than a dozen people ran it, with the admirable precision only a small group of long-time co-workers can achieve. This small administrative structure was possible basically because the social workers were an elite group, well educated—all of them having earned the M.S.W. degree—thoroughly experienced, and well paid. Given light caseloads and access to the resources they needed for their young clients, they were expected to do an outstanding job. This parallel with Jim Casey's philosophy in managing UPS was not, of course, accidental.

By 1972 the distinct success of Casey's program encouraged a major expansion, and the resources of the Annie E. Casey Foundation were sufficient to underwrite such an effort. But, rather than expanding in western Washington and risking disruption of an apparatus that functioned so effectively, Casey and the board of trustees decided to create new "divisions" of similar size and structure in places that needed The Casey Family Program. They chose to avoid the layers of vertical structure that would have accompanied expansion of the Seattle organization and instead opted for the decentralized mode of operation that had served UPS so well. To them it seemed the appropriate way to proceed for an organization having service as its primary goal.

Consequently, a second division of The Casey Family Program opened in Yakima, Washington, in 1972, followed almost immediately by a division in Boise, Idaho. The Montana Division, with headquarters in Helena, began operations early in 1973, followed by California in 1973, Oregon in 1977, South Dakota in 1980, North Dakota, Arizona, and Hawaii in 1983, and Oklahoma, Texas (Austin and San Antonio), and Wyoming in 1987.

Establishing new divisions was the specialty of George Fahey. He would visit a community that had expressed interest in the Program and seek information from a cross section of its leaders about the area's needs, about talented individuals who might be willing to serve on the advisory committee of a new division, and about the ways in which their community was unique and might need different features in its foster care program.

Fahey's aim in each case was to take the model successfully developed in Seattle and apply it in a new community, but with modifications that were appropriate to conditions in that community. A new division was never a clone of the original, but markedly resembled the original in structure, operation, and goals.

Once a new division had its advisory committee, the committee's first task was to hire an experienced foster care professional, with excellent training and administrative ability, to hire social workers and direct the operations of the division. Master's-level social workers from strong university programs were sought for both director and professional staff, but their most important qualities would be responsibility and a strong ethical sense. The program used periodic accreditation by state agencies and the Child Welfare League of America to ensure that care met the highest standards, but from the managerial point of view, high-quality care was seen as the product of a long-term relationship between social workers and the Program. Division directors recruited workers who could make commitments in terms of decades rather than years. Workers received good pay, respect, and very reasonable caseloads. In return, they were expected to concern themselves with the long-term as well as the day-to-day interests of their clients and the Program.

Once formed, new divisions had substantial latitude to develop their own versions of The Casey Family Program model of foster care. They were hardly set adrift, however. The most experienced of the Program's professionals provided training and guidance. Moreover, communication between Carl Erickson, who became the first executive director, and division directors was frequent and structured.

Division directors were expected to use the time and talents of their social workers efficiently and to be knowledgeable about every child assigned to the division. The division kept comprehensive case records for each child in care, kept financial records ready for audit at any time, and regularly monitored the overall situation of each foster family.

Initially, of course, every new division found itself with two principal tasks. The first was locating children in need of the planned, long-term care The Casey Family Program provided, which required developing a network of relationships with state, local, and private agencies, the courts, service directors, politicians, clergy, and involved lay persons.

The network, once in place, frequently provided tips that helped with the second major task, locating good foster families. But most divisions came to rely primarily on a "foster home developer," a staff person hired to seek out, sound out, and investigate potential foster families. In some divisions a desirable family might move through three layers of assessment: the foster home developer, the division director, and the director plus professional staff. In others, the foster home developer might steer the family at once to a full meeting with the director and staff.

In the assessment, many areas of foster parent functioning were probed. In the Montana Division, to give a specific and fairly representative example, there were 15 particular areas of concern. More or less in order of importance, they were:

Ability to tolerate frustrations and keep commitments

Skills in problem solving—for example, the ability to analyze behavior and test ideas about it

Degree of comfort with the Program and with using social work services and the services of other professional persons

Understanding of and experience with children

Ability to deal with separation, loss, and emancipation

Support from extended family, friends, and others for undertaking foster care

Motivation

Rigidity or flexibility of personality

Marital relationship

Pattern of communication

Ability to teach

Maturity of the foster parents

Ability to accept a foster child's biological family

Ability to individualize children

Emancipation experience of the foster parents from their own families

Casey Family professionals in Montana like to summarize these qualities by saying that they look for loving and caring foster parents who project a "tough kindness." These potential parents must be good problem solvers who can relate to separation and loss and, thus, to the very deprived children the Program makes its top priority.

These children are often ones whom potential foster families would not choose to provide care for, even given the strongest intrinsic motivation. Jim Casey understood this difficulty and made financial incentive and continuing support one of the keystones of his program. Foster families receive a monthly stipend for each foster child, as well as allowances for clothing, school expenses, and the like. The Program also pays for the child's health care and special needs. These special needs can range from educational tutoring to physical therapy to psychotherapy to (in selected cases) brief institutional care.

The costs of special services are not as high as might be expected, given the troubled pasts of most of the Program's children. The moderate-to high-intensity service the social workers provide lessens the need for outside practitioners. Although their professional styles vary from extremely nondirective to confronting, the social workers make a special point of being present when their foster families need them, and of anticipating these periods of need. In most divisions, the entire professional staff can mobilize itself within hours to handle a crisis in one of its foster families. Social workers in some divisions have extensive training in psychotherapy and routinely handle severe problems on their own, although backup specialists are available and used if needed.

Because The Casey Family Program (TCFP) provides long-term care and because the foster children tend to remain with one family for many years, stable and predictable relationships develop. Even the disruptions tend to take on a pattern, making crisis management a more containable problem. As in all programs of foster care, however, some Casey Family children do run away, some commit criminal offenses, some fail academically, and some are returned to the custody of the courts, state social welfare systems, and their biological families. Yet given that many of the Program's foster children come from backgrounds impoverished in almost every way, the success rate is high.

This success appears to result mainly from the planned, long-term care. Not only can problems be foreseen and forestalled, but also some unexpected dividends accrue. Families and children begin to orient toward the agency as a stable factor in their lives. Every division has its complement of "Casey-long term" families—especially good caregivers who tend to provide homes for several TCFP children over the years. And sometimes a child who has been unable to establish a permanent relationship with any foster family comes to regard the agency and the division social workers as the stable center of his or her life. Although one might decry the emotional poverty assumed by a child's having an agency as a parental figure, it is clearly more desirable than the possible alternatives for many of the children The Casey Family Program has taken on.

Again, planned care from beginning to end is the central concept in the Casey system. A child's first visit to a potential foster family, for example, is carefully orchestrated. The visit is long enough for people to get to know one another but not long enough for unfamiliar behavior patterns to cause friction. The foster parents know what to expect from the foster child who, in turn, knows what to expect of the family. Neither is put on best behavior. Both are counseled that any family relationship is imperfect in some ways and that compromise is not only necessary but healthy.

Planning and coordinating a foster child's experiences extend to his or her schooling, to the predictable difficulties of adolescence, to initial experiences with independent living, and finally to emancipation and beyond. As far as possible, the foster families share in all of this. The Casey Family Program not only involves them as counselors and consultants where their own foster child is concerned, it also gathers them for workshops where knowledgeable and often distinguished professionals provide insights into child management techniques. It invites them to professional gatherings of child welfare organizations, to observe and/or participate in sessions that address their concerns.

The Program has invested an increasing proportion of its effort and resources in emancipation. As foster children approach majority, social workers assess their educational, motivational, and emotional assets. With careful consultations, they help the young persons choose among post-high school possibilities. Should they choose education or an apprenticeship, the Student Aid Program can finance training through the doctoral level or its equivalent. When an alternative such as an army career is more appropriate, the social worker helps clarify advantages and drawbacks.

Aware that a young person's first choice may not be the best one or may not for other reasons work out, the agency is ready to provide as much additional help as the young person will accept. Such a matter can, of course, become complicated because of the right to privacy and freedom from intrusion any adult deserves. The desire of a former foster child to distance himself or herself from the agency is always respected.

We have provided this bare-bones outline of the history and functioning of The Casey Family Program as a basis for understanding the material in the next chapters. Those chapters contain vignettes of actual Casey Family children in interactions with the agency and their foster families. These, we hope, will flesh out the bones.

2

Study I   The Montana Division
Study

In this chapter we begin by discussing the origins of our three studies for The Casey Family Program, factors that influenced the form of the first study, and what that study was intended to accomplish. The remainder of the chapter describes the sample of foster children who constituted the subjects of the first study, the sources and domains of information we had available to draw on concerning them, and the kinds of outcomes we tried to predict for them.

The domains of information are described in detail, because it is the richness and abundance of information available about foster children in TCFP that allowed us to make a genuinely wide-ranging search for factors associated with desirable placement outcomes.

Background

The Casey Family Program specializes in providing foster care for children from particularly disadvantaged backgrounds. Factors such as severe marital discord between the parents, overcrowding in the home, a psychiatric disorder in the mother, criminal activities by the father, and episodes of institutional care for the child are commonplace in their history. Research such as Rutter's[1] has demonstrated that children with more than one such risk factor in their background are at least four times as likely to fall prey to serious emotional, intellectual, and social problems than less threatened children. As Garmezy[2] has demonstrated, however, some children beset by serious stress and disruptive influences display every sign of psychological well-being and appear able to cope with difficulties that would disable most of their peers. Among the factors that characterize such "superchildren" are the ability to attract and use adult support, a high degree of autonomy and ego strength, and both traditional (such as school grades and Scouting and Campfire awards) and creative achievements.

The Montana Division of TCFP was one of many groups that became interested in Garmezy's research in the late 1970s. Its staff reasoned that if behaviors that allowed children with superior adaptive capacity to overcome obstacles could be better identified, and if practical techniques for enhancing these behaviors could be developed, the knowledge could be used to increase the chances that foster children in the Program would achieve a normal and productive adulthood.

During the late 1970s the authors were also engaged in research involving superchildren. We were attempting to develop behavioral measures of variables associated with superior adaptive capacity. A colleague who was aware of our interests and those of TCFP introduced us to the Montana staff. The similarity of focus of our efforts became apparent, and we began to discuss strategies for identifying elements of superchild behavior by means of standard behavioral assessment techniques and brief, naturalistically oriented observational methods.

In exploring the resources available to develop these strategies, however, two things became apparent. First, the Montana Division possessed almost an embarrassment of riches in terms of information about its foster children. This information went far beyond factors that might lead to superior adaptive capacity and pertained to almost every aspect of the children's lives, from their earliest years right up to the present. Second, superior adaptive capacity was a means and not an end; that is, enhancing superchild behaviors was not a goal in itself; the main point was maintenance of promising foster placements. Children who were able to maintain their placement in a foster family over several years appeared much more likely to achieve emancipation into successful adult lives than children whose placements were brief, marked by turmoil, and generally unsuccessful.

The Problem

The focus of our efforts underwent a major shift as we realized that within the archives of the Montana Division there might exist information that could be used to predict the outcomes of foster placements. A

LILLY

Lilly is 14, tall and still young-girl-slim and bony. She is Native American, the second of three children having the same mother but different fathers. The children have been placed together in one home, that of an urban Native American couple.

Lilly has one older sister and one younger brother. Their mother is seriously mentally ill and since their births the children have sometimes lived with her, sometimes with relatives, sometimes together, sometimes not. When Lilly was ten, the children were taken from their mother because she had deteriorated to the point of neglecting as well as abusing them. They were taken on as Casey Family children, and because they had been their own most stable family, it was decided to try to keep them together.

The money TCFP provides for the children is crucial to the foster household, since the foster father and mother are only occasionally able to find employment. Both foster parents consider making a home for the children their jobs, however, and they are conscientious about it. They encourage good progress in school, but also take the children to powwows and have incorporated them into their own extended families.

Lilly is probably the most intelligent of the siblings, but she is also the most shy and uncertain. This is partly due to her age, but it is also due to her being discriminated against by her sister and brother. Their fathers were of the same tribe as their mother, but Lilly's father was of a tribe looked down upon by the others, and she is taunted with that; however, her foster parents are aware of the problem and try to minimize the damage to her. When she first came to live with them, Lilly was extremely passive and unreactive, but the four years of stability she has enjoyed and the chance to shine academically have been good for her. She stands up for herself now. And if at the moment she wants to become the world's greatest roller skater, she is also making rather more practical plans for herself. Knowing that with TCFP help she can continue her education, she wants to go to college and become a nurse.

systematic search for factors apparently associated with placement maintenance elicited some factors that appeared to characterize the child as a unique individual, others that seemed to originate in the background and behavior of the biological family, and still others that were associated with the foster parents and the makeup and functioning of their home.

As we examined in detail the placement history of a number of foster children, it became clear that particular, quite specific factors and combinations of factors were consistently predictive of stable placements, while other combinations of variables indicated the likelihood of brief and unsuccessful placements. It was apparent as well that the degree to which a given variable predicted placement outcome depended in a relatively complex way on which other factors were present and to what degree.

At this point we began to consider formal predictive models in which factors are weighted in terms of their importance and summed to provide an overall index of placement success. Various statistical techniques of this kind are available. Standard multiple regression analysis, discriminant function analysis, and survival analysis were considered as possible predictive systems. Pilot efforts convinced us that a standard multiple regression approach probably offered the most informative results, given the available data. We made the decision to try to derive a multiple regression equation relating factors that could (at least in principle) be known at the time a child was placed in a foster home to the occurrence of placement breakdown while the child was in foster care with TCFP.

Although a majority of the predictors had their roots in the concerns routinely raised with prospective foster families, as mentioned in Chapter 1, we made it a point to include any factor that held out any promise whatever of adding to the predictability of placement maintenance. We were aware that we were thus engaged in a type of shotgun empiricism, but we took statistical steps, for example, conservative levels of significance, and also more general methodological measures, such as cross-validation, to help protect ourselves from misleading conclusions.

The Sample

Before specifying exactly what information about each child would be tallied, we considered which children under care in the Montana Division should be included in the study. Since we wanted the results to describe as generally as possible the relationship between potential predictive factors and placement maintenance in the Montana Division, we decided to include every child currently in care for whom substantially complete data were available.

The Montana Division had 50 children in care when we began data collection early in 1980. Essentially complete information was available on 47 of these individuals. Three others were the product of such confused and chaotic backgrounds that many facts concerning their early lives and families were either unknown or highly speculative. To the 47 children for whom complete data were available were added four others whose records were intact and who had been participants in the Program recently enough that its mode of operation at that time was comparable to what was being done in 1980.

Thus, the sample comprised 51 children. Their backgrounds and personal characteristics were remarkably varied. Before going into detail about them, however, we will describe the sources and domains of information available to us and the processes by which the data were obtained, refined, edited, and recorded.

Data Sources

The main data source was the archives of the Montana Division of TCFP. Although the total data storage system was complex, we will from now on refer simply to "case files." One of the categories of information the case files contained was biological family histories. Some had been obtained from one of the parents, or from an aunt, uncle, cousin, grandparent, or a more remote relation; others were compilations and codifications of information from two or more family members. Occasionally they consisted largely of investigative summaries by private or public social service agencies or the courts. Most of them were highly detailed, but unless the details were known with a substantial degree of certainty, they were not tallied for purposes of analysis.

In addition to family records, the files contained medical, social, and psychiatric information. They included placement histories, descriptions of developmental trends, summaries of school experiences, interactions with judicial and social agencies, and, from the time a child was accepted by TCFP, monthly (or more frequent) narrative reports of the child's behavior and circumstances.

The case files were also rich in information about the foster family (or families) with which a child had been placed after admission to The Casey Family Program. Demographic, financial, social, and attitudinal data were available, as well as descriptions of personalities, patterns of interaction, and significant persons and events in the histories of these foster families.

In 1979 Margaret Stuart, a member of the social work faculty at Carroll College, worked with a somewhat different subset of case files and summarized and systematized information on the foster children under several headings, three of which were of considerable use to the present investigators: (1) placement history; (2) relationship and developmental factors that had had important effects on a child's life; and (3) factors likely to have put a child at risk with respect to mental illness, antisocial behavior, educational delay or failure, and in attaching or establishing and maintaining relationships.

The final and in many ways most useful source of information was caseworker ratings. Because of their close and long-standing relationships with both foster children and foster families (and sometimes with the biological families as well), the caseworkers were prolific sources of sophisticated, professional assessments of personality characteristics of individuals, of abilities ranging from reading achievement to social skills, of interest patterns, motives, habits, and, most notably, of foster family behavioral repertoires, styles, capacities, and resources. The judgments and assessments of the workers were not accepted uncritically, but, as will be described below, they proved to be both useful and dependable.

Domains of Information

After eliminating obviously redundant questions, we retained 282 items of information about each child. "Obviously redundant" is an important phrase, because it was not always apparent that similar-looking items supplied identical information. We asked, for example, whether there was evidence of serious neglect by the mother in the child's early life. We also asked, because it seemed to us a distinct question, whether there was evidence that the neglect per se had put the child substantially at risk in terms of subsequent overall adjustment. Whether or not the two questions were, in fact, distinct within the context of this study was assumed to be an empirical matter to be decided by our analytical methods.

Because the contents of each case file were to some extent unique, and different details were known with varying degrees of certainty, not every item of information was recorded for every child. The most complete file yielded data on 274 items out of 282; the most incomplete provided information on 246 items. On the average, there were about ten items per child about which the case file was not informative.

The items have been grouped into ten domains as a means of imposing some conceptual organization on the large data set that was created. To provide a convenient mode of reference, they are named as follows, and each has a short abbreviation listed in parentheses.

    I.   Personal characteristics of the foster child (PC)

   II.   Demographic characteristics of the foster child (DC)

  III.   The foster child's characteristic responses to threat (RT)

  IV.   History of the biological family (NF)

   V.   Serious risk factors in the foster child's history (RF)

  VI.   Placement history (PH)

 VII.   Present placement situation (PP)

VIII.   Characteristics of the present foster family (PF)

  IX.   Factors involved in placement breakdown while in TCFP (PB)

   X.   Caseworker's professional orientation (PO)

In separate tables below are listed the items in the ten domains. Because some items could reasonably be placed in more than one domain, and because some placements were made on *a priori* logical grounds

while others were made for empirical reasons, the location of a few items
is somewhat arbitrary. The reader should not be distracted by this fact:
analysis of the relationship of an item to placement breakdown while in
the Program proceeded in the same way for every item, regardless of the
domain to which it was assigned for conceptual purposes.

The items in the tables are numbered sequentially, and it will occasionally be useful to refer to them by these numbers. When this is done,
they will be identified by means of their domain abbreviation.

Domain I   Personal Characteristics of the Foster Child

The items in Domain I are primarily caseworkers' ratings of some
eye-catching aspects of personality, maladaptive behavior, coping mechanisms, and appearance (Table 1). Because they were highly characteristic of
particular children whose placements had differed markedly in how successful they had been, we felt that they were potentially useful predictors
of maintenance. There are also three items from the case files concerning
hobbies. Some possible redundancy is apparent here in that PC-19 asks
about musical and athletic skills, whereas PC-24 and PC-25 ask about
musical and athletic hobbies. The obvious factor that differentiates these
items is the caseworker's judgment about whether the child possessed
some ability in a musical or athletic area in addition to exhibiting the long-
term interest and involvement that would classify an activity as a hobby.

The items in this domain are eye-catchers in that they were aspects of
the foster children in the Montana Division that caused one or more
individuals to stand out from their peers. Several children, for example,
were noteworthy for being well groomed and dressed, whereas others
were equally noteworthy for their consistently sloppy or disheveled appearance. Several seemed to cultivate a street urchin style of dress (at a
time when this fashion was not stylish among the young) that nothing in
their present family or financial circumstances made necessary. Most of
the items in Domain I were based, however, not on physical appearance
but on personality variables of the sort delineated by Henry Murray[3] and
formalized in current inventories such as Jackson's *Personality Research
Form,*[4] or on behaviors and coping mechanisms of the kind associated
with personality disorders, as described in the *Diagnostic and Statistical
Manual*[5] of the American Psychiatric Association.

A great many items of these sorts were considered as possible predictors of placement maintenance. Most were eventually discarded. The
ones that were retained were those that (1) were thought to characterize at

least one child in ten in the sample; *(2)* could be defined in unambiguous terms that included specific behavioral indicators; and *(3)* were typically exhibited over a relatively long time period, that is, six months or more. (Some of these items were placed in Domain III, because they were considered to be primarily responses to threat; they will be discussed below.)

Several of these items require clarification. PC-3 does not refer to a child's achievement only in school, but in his or her entire life situation. In PC-14, "pseudomature" refers to a child's presenting a facade of mature and responsible reaction to life problems but not actually possessing the degree of psychological integration that the facade would imply. "Seductive" in PC-18 is a label not for sexual seductiveness, but for a willingness to trade apparent entrée to the child's inner thoughts and feelings in return for attention and time spent together. "Initiates rescue complex" in PC-22 refers to the ability to project such a strong need to be removed from one's present difficulties that an adult who is in contact with the child finds himself or herself involved in a rescue without really having considered whether such an effort is either appropriate or useful. The phrasing of these items is to some extent telegraphic and idiosyncratic, but was employed to convey complex ideas in a reasonably compact fashion.

Domain II   Demographic Characteristics of the Foster Child

The items in Domain II cover the demographic facts of age, race, and religion (Table 2). They are often good predictors of social phenomena, and we wished to test their relevance to placement maintenance. Among other possibilities, we wanted to see whether a child's gender was associated with placement stability, since more of the girls than the boys under care in the Montana Division seemed to thrive in their foster settings. We were also interested in whether race was by itself a determinant of placement outcome.

The asterisks next to items DC-1, DC-3, DC-4, and DC-5 indicate that when these data were coded for analysis they were reclassified as binary indicators to clarify their meaning and facilitate their interpretation. Thus, DC-1 consisted of three distinct items when the data on a particular child were coded. He or she was identified as Caucasian or not, Native American or not, or some other (or unknown) race or not. These binary indicators were obviously not independent of each other, but multiple regression does not require complete independence as long as no predic-

TABLE 1

Domain I   Personal Characteristics of the Foster Child (PC)

Item

Child is/has . . .

1. curious and/or inquisitive
2. passive-aggressive
3. a low achiever
4. charming and/or expressive
5. unique, one-of-a-kind
6. extremely needy of affection
7. manipulative
8. afraid of intimacy
9. anxious and fearful
10. low self-esteem
11. unable to deal with success
12. impulsive
13. low frustration tolerance
14. pseudomature
15. good social skills
16. physically attractive
17. likeable
18. seductive
19. athletic, musical, or similar skill
20. waif or street urchin appearance
21. a significant hobby
22. one who initiates rescue complex
23. one who dresses and grooms neatly
24. hobby of music
25. hobby of sports

tor is completely reproducible from another predictor or subset of predictors.[a]

Age (DC-2) is a variable we felt certain would be associated with placement maintenance, with younger children being generally better risks. But it was considered possible that because different developmental tasks assume more importance at one time period than another, children in one of three five-year age ranges (6–10, 11–15, 16–20) might be inherently more at risk for placement breakdown within The Casey Family Program framework. Thus, foster children between six and 20 were

[a] Occasionally items had to be deleted in the course of an analysis to avoid such "collinearity."

TABLE 2

Domain II   Demographic Characteristics of the Foster Child (DC)

Item

Child . . .
*1.   is Caucasian, Native American, other, unknown
 2.   is _____ years of age
*3.   falls in age range 6–10 years, 11–15 years, 16–20 years
*4.   is male/female
*5.   has religious affiliation of Catholic, Mormon, Protestant, other, none

classified as belonging to one of the three ranges. The resulting three binary indicators were then used as predictor variables.

Finally, it has been argued that some religious groups provide a framework that encourages family stability to a greater degree than others. We wished to review the evidence for such an effect within the Montana Division sample.

More complete breakdowns of racial/ethnic background and religious affiliation could have been accomplished on the basis of available information, but a total of only four or five children would have been included in the seven or eight additional binary categories, and trial analyses indicated that the additional categories did not produce clearer results. Only breakdowns and categories capturing 5 percent or more of the total sample were retained for the final analysis.

Domain III   The Foster Child's Characteristic Responses to Threat

Domain III consists of characteristic responses to threat identified by Margaret Stuart in her analysis of foster children in the Montana Division of The Casey Family Program. Different combinations of responses to threat appeared to characterize so many children so uniquely that we felt they had great potential as a predictor of placement breakdown or change (Table 3). Some of these responses to threat had much of the character of ego defense mechanisms, and many were also frequently employed by the foster child to control the foster family. The behaviors associated with some of these defenses were among the aspects of the children most frequently and most strongly objected to by their foster families. The behaviors are often mentioned in the *Diagnostic and Statistical Manual* in

TABLE 3

Domain III   The Foster Child's Characteristic Responses to Threat (RT)

Item

Child's response to threat is . . .
1. aggression or violence
2. passive-aggressive behavior
3. disobedience or resistance
4. distancing
5. wetting or soiling
6. phobic behavior
7. anger or hostility
8. running away
9. being withdrawn or moody
10. acting out
11. overcompensation
12. suppression
13. lying or deceiving
14. attention seeking
15. pseudomaturity
16. defensiveness
17. hyperactivity
18. other
19. no unusual activity

association with disorders of childhood and especially in connection with personality disorders.

The "other" category in RT-18 was used to characterize a varied set of rare behaviors, such as fetishism, which had a total frequency in the sample of just over 5 percent. "No unusual activity" (RT-19) was included to see whether the relatively small number of children with no characteristic response to threat were more likely to maintain stable placements than those with one or more such responses. Similar items were used for analogous purposes in other domains.

Domain IV   History of the Biological Family

The family was a primary influence on the behavior of Montana Division children, and Domain IV concentrates on the existence of relatives of all degrees and the child's contacts or lack of contacts with them as potential predictors of placement maintenance (Table 4).

The experience of Montana Division caseworkers indicated that the greater the number of relatives known to the child, the greater their number of contacts with the child, and the longer the period over which the contacts had occurred, the more likely it was that the child would maintain a stable placement.

The mother and father are, of course, of special importance, and even their symbolic presence, that is, the child knowing them to be alive, or living in Montana, seemed to be related to greater stability. Abuse, neglect, alcoholism, and mental illnesses appeared to be factors that attenuated their influence, while a close early attachment strengthened it.

The child's relationship to the father appeared to be especially complex. Because fathers were often shadowy, rather mysterious background figures, knowledge of them assumed unusual significance for the child, who might, for example, take a perverse but real pride in the fact that the father had had a criminal background.

Domain V Serious Risk Factors in the Foster Child's History

Domain V sets forth serious risk factors in the foster child's history, especially in her or his early experience. These risk factors had obvious and often severe effects on the lives of many Montana Division children and seemed to offer considerable promise as predictors of placement maintenance (Table 5).

The first 20 items in this domain represent factors judged to have put foster children in the Montana Division seriously at risk with respect to mental illness, antisocial behavior, educational delay or failure, and establishing or maintaining relationships.

The death or serious illness of one or both parents, or abuse, desertion, and/or neglect created the most serious risks, but family disruption, substance abuse, battering, incarceration of a parent, and similar factors were frequent pointers toward poor outcomes. Several specific combinations of factors, for example, abuse and/or neglect and/or poor nurturance or incompetent care by the mother, as in RF-5, occurred with considerable frequency and were used as single indicators to determine whether such combinations produced an interaction that was greater than the sum of their parts.

RF-19 was used in a manner similar to RT-18, that is, to characterize a varied set of low-frequency behaviors, the very unusualness of which was considered to be of possible predictive significance.

As the superchild literature makes clear, some children have resources that enable them to triumph over a potentially disabling environ-

TABLE 4

Domain IV   History of the Biological Family (NF)

Item

With respect to parents . . .
1. both parents are known
2. parents are divorced
3. one or both parents is/are deceased
    Mother . . .
4. was _____ years of age at the birth of this child
5. was 22 years of age or younger at the birth of this child
6. has current whereabouts that are known
7. is known to live in Montana
8. currently has no contact and no involvement with the child
9. currently has some contact with the child
10. is known to have been mentally ill, and/or to have had an alcohol abuse problem, and/or to have committed suicide
11. is currently hospitalized or institutionalized
12. is known to have felt close to the child, and/or to have had a close attachment to the child, and/or to have given the child a great deal of affection
13. is known to have rejected and/or abused and/or neglected and/or deserted the child
    Father . . .
14. is not known
15. was _____ years of age at the birth of this child
16. has currently unknown whereabouts
17. is known to live in Montana
18. currently has no contact and no involvement with the child
19. currently has some contact with the child
20. is known to have had an alcohol abuse problem
21. is known to have had a criminal record
22. is known to have been hospitalized or to be deceased
23. is known to have abused the child
24. is known to have failed to accept the child, and/or to have had no relationship with the child, and/or to have rejected the child
    With respect to siblings, child . . .
25. has no siblings or half-siblings
26. has one or more siblings or half-siblings
27. has one or more siblings within five years of own age
28. has shared a home at some time with one or more siblings
29. has one or more siblings who lives with parents
30. is known to have had a close relationship with at least one sibling
31. is known to have had a poor relationship or rivalry with one or more siblings
32. has frequent contact with one or more siblings

TABLE 4—Continued

33. has sporadic contact with one or more siblings
34. has no contact with any siblings
35. has no records or other information concerning siblings
36. has scant records or no information about relationships with siblings
    With respect to other relatives . . .
37. grandparents are known to have been significant figures in the child's past
38. aunts, uncles, cousins are known to have been significant figures in the child's past
39. child has important relatives other than parents or siblings
40. no relatives other than siblings are known to have been significant figures in child's past
41. frequent or continuing contacts with relatives other than siblings have occurred
42. sporadic contacts with relatives other than siblings have occurred
43. child has no present contacts with relatives other than siblings

ment, and the ability to form and maintain relationships appears to be such a resource. We made it a special point to address the ability of each foster child in this respect, as in RF-21.

Finally, many of these items are clearly a matter of family history. They are included here rather than in Domain IV because they so often seemed to be precursors of serious problems such as mental illness.

Domain VI   Placement History

Domain VI provides detailed placement history considered to be particularly salient to placement stability (Table 6). Because age at first placement, especially if it occurred before six years of age, seemed to be an excellent predictor of placement maintenance, we began with it, but also checked whether five-year ranges of age at first placement were predictive of more or less stable placements.

The nature of the first placement, with relatives as opposed to a receiving home, for example, was examined, as were the various reasons for the first placement. Many of these reasons have some overlap with both risk factors and history of the family, but they were retained because of the possibly unique information that the impetus for initial placement outside the child's own home might provide.

The number of placements of all sorts following the first one was thoroughly examined because of the general and well-known finding that a large number of early placements indicates a poor prognosis for later ones.

TABLE 5

Domain V   Serious Risk Factors in the Foster Child's History (RF)

Item

Child was . . .
1. rejected by mother
2. rejected by father
3. deserted by mother
4. deserted by father
5. abused and/or not nurtured and/or neglected and/or provided incompetent care by mother
    Child was put at risk by . . .
6. mother's illness/death/suicide
7. father's illness/death/suicide
8. disruption of or turmoil in family
9. separation from siblings
10. physical or emotional abuse by parent(s) or caregiver(s)
11. neglect by caregiver
12. financial stress upon parent(s) or other caregiver(s)
13. the incarceration of a parent
14. alcohol problems in the family
15. physical violence among members of the family
16. divorce of parents
17. family's frequent moves from one household or geographical location to another
18. inconsistent discipline by parent(s) or other caregiver(s)
19. other factors
20. failure of early foster placements
    Child's level of risk . . .
21. was alleviated by ability to form and maintain relationships

We wanted to know whether there was an overall increase in risk of placement breakdown as number of previous placements increased over the wide range presented in this sample. We also recorded occurrence of an institutional placement, which is another bellwether of later placement failure.

We tried to take an approach to categorizing child-related reasons for placement breakdown that was reasonably comprehensive but limited to behaviors that occurred with sufficient frequency to have some prognostic generality. We attempted a similar approach to listing risk factors in subsequent foster placements. We were, of course, interested in factors that were common to placement breakdowns among the very deprived children TCFP serves.

TABLE 6

Domain VI Placement History (PH)

Item

1. Child's age at first placement was _____ years
   Child was . . .
2. 0–5 years of age at first placement
3. 6–10 years of age at first placement
4. 11 years of age or older at first placement
   Child's first placement outside the own home was . . .
5. with relatives or family friends
6. in foster care
7. receiving
8. in an institution
9. in a setting other than those listed above
   Reason for child's first placement outside the own home was . . .
10. death of parent(s)
11. health of parent(s)
12. some combination of death of one parent and poor health of the other
13. desertion of parent(s)
14. relinquishment by parent(s)
15. family disruption
16. some combination of desertion, relinquishment, disruption, abuse
17. behavior problems
18. Number of placements outside the home subsequent to the first is _____
    Child had . . .
19. 0–5 placements subsequent to the first
20. 6–10 placements subsequent to the first
21. 11–15 placements subsequent to the first
22. more than 15 placements subsequent to the first
23. one or more sets of stepparents before the current parents
24. one or more placement(s) in institution(s)
    Child-related reason for placement breakdown(s) before enrollment in TCFP was . . .
25. acting out, including firesetting and/or stealing and/or substance abuse and/or aggression and/or violence and/or sexual acting out
26. anger and/or hostility and/or withdrawal
27. hyperactivity
28. inability of foster parents to cope with the child
29. passive-aggressive behavior
30. running away
31. failure to integrate with the foster family
32. inability to cope with authority
33. tantrums

TABLE 6—Continued

34. being untrustworthy
     *Risk factor in placements outside the own home subsequent to the first
     was . . .*
35. health problems
36. school problems
37. many moves
38. physical and/or emotional abuse
39. rejection by foster parents or custodians
40. acting-out behavior
41. failure to attach
42. peer interaction problems
43. separation from previous foster parents
44. death of biological parents or previous foster parents
45. foster family disruption
46. abuse by stepfather
47. nature of the placements themselves
48. some factor other than those listed above
     Final separation . . .
49. from the parents has occurred
50. from parents occurred _____ years ago

Domain VII   Present Placement Situation

Domain VII deals with very specific aspects of the foster child's present placement situation. Several of these items were included to generate summary descriptions of the sample rather than as predictors of maintenance, since they pertained to an existing placement (Table 7).

If the child was temporarily not in foster care, we determined whether he or she was in a group home, quasi-independent care, an institution, or some interim situation. The child's general geographic location in the state was recorded as a possible source of variation in type or intensity of care.

Given the evolution of the Montana Division, the year of acceptance into the program was also considered as possibly being associated with placement stability. For example, some of the earliest children accepted had some of the most deprived backgrounds.

Minority group membership and placement in a minority home were recorded, as was continuing contact with family members and whether the child had siblings in TCFP.

TABLE 7

Domain VII   Present Placement Situation (PP)

Item

Child is . . .
1. not presently in foster care
2. in a group home
3. in private residential care
4. in a public institution
5. in quasi-independent care
6. in interim care
7. in the Scholarship Program
8. not in contact with agency
9. placed in a minority home (if a minority group member)
10. placed in a nonminority home (if a minority group member)
11. located in the Helena area
12. located in the Great Falls area
13. located in the Missoula area
14. located in another area in Montana
15. located outside Montana
    Child was accepted by the Program . . .
16. in 1975 or before
17. in 1976 or 1977
18. in 1978 or later
19. in the year ____
20. when he or she was _____ years of age
    Child has . . .
21. ongoing contact with mother
22. sporadic contact with mother
23. ongoing contact with father
24. sporadic contact with father
25. no siblings in the Program
26. one sibling in the Program
27. more than one sibling in the Program
    Agency has . . .
28. contact with mother
29. contact with father

Domain VIII   Characteristics of the Present Foster Family

Domain VIII covers characteristics of the present foster family that the experience of The Casey Family Program indicated were among the most important determiners of placement success (Table 8).

CARY

Cary is a tall, thin, rather undistinguished looking 16-year-old. He is the only foster child in a large Catholic family whose eight children range in age from six to 22.

Cary lived with his unmarried mother until he was six years old. At that time, unemployed and emotionally unable to care for him, his mother deserted him. The state placed him in a series of foster homes. With each placement breakdown he became more sullen and stubborn. He began to run away when he was about nine. He had periodic contact with his mother, but she didn't seem to be able to make a stable life for herself and showed no interest in trying to make one for him.

Cary came to the attention of The Casey Family Program when he was 11. He was placed by them with a family living on a large ranch close to the city where Cary's mother lived. The family had not taken foster children before, but they felt a strong commitment toward trying to improve the world. They also had a son very close to Cary's age and hoped the companionship would be good for both boys.

Cary has been with the family for five years, and they consider him one of their children. The discipline the parents have always maintained with their own children has been very beneficial for Cary. He came to them with a strong disinclination for work of any kind, physical or mental, but he has been expected to help with the chores and to perform as well as possible in school. Since all the children have been expected to do the same, and he was not singled out, he eventually learned to do what was expected, though he has never developed real enthusiasm for it.

His foster family includes Cary in all its family outings, and he attends church services and activities with them. His foster family has been scrupulous about not influencing him on the matter, but he has decided on his own to become confirmed in the Catholic church.

Whether the companionship with the foster brother his age has worked out is something of a question. Being of the same age, they are often in competitive situations. His foster brother resents the fact that his place in the family must be shared. He also resents TCFP money that gives Cary some extras that he doesn't have. At the same time, Cary resents the fact that his foster brother is a harder worker and somewhat more successful academically than Cary.

Cary's biological mother has married and has had two more children. Her life is more stable, and Cary spends two weeks of each summer with her. But Cary doesn't seem to want or expect to return to her (nor does she offer him a home). His foster family really has become his family.

The first consideration was certain basic characteristics of the foster mother and foster father: age, birth order, education, and employment, including job security. A tentative hypothesis was that older foster parents who had been middle children, who were better educated and had better jobs with greater security, would be more successful in maintaining placements. We were interested in the emotional coherence of the foster

TABLE 8

Domain VIII   Characteristics of the Present Foster Family (PF)

Item

Foster mother . . .
1. is _____ years of age
2. in terms of birth order is herself an oldest, intermediate, or youngest child
3. has an educational level of: less than high school, high school, some college, college, college plus additional training
4. works outside the home
5. has good job security, if works outside the home
6. is in the process of liberation
7. provides a strong female role model in the foster family
8. possesses strong emotional coherence
9. has earth mother as her dominant personal style
10. initiated taking the foster child into the home
    Foster father . . .
11. is _____ years of age.
12. in terms of birth order is himself an oldest, intermediate, or youngest child
13. has an educational level of: less than high school, high school, some college, college, college plus additional training
14. works outside the home
15. has good job security, if works outside the home
16. provides a strong male role model in the foster family
17. is emotionally involved with the child
18. initiated taking the foster child into the home
    With respect to mix of children in the foster home . . .
19. the foster child is younger than all of the foster family's own children
20. the foster child is intermediate in age with respect to the own children
21. the foster child is older than all of the own children
22. the number of own children living at home is _____
23. the number of preschool own children living at home is _____
24. the foster family has experience with the age group of the foster child
    With respect to their marriage . . .
25. the foster parents have been married _____ years
26. one or both foster parents have been married previously
27. the foster parents made a commitment to child-rearing early in their marriage
28. the foster parents viewed taking the child into their home as a new phase of child-rearing
29. the foster parents took the child into their home in an attempt to avoid starting a new phase of marriage
30. the foster parents have encouraged a physically affectionate family style
31. the foster parents exhibit a high degree of comfort in their several roles

TABLE 8—Continued

32. the foster parents' personal interaction is one of ease
    With respect to communication and problem-solving skills . . .
33. the foster family has the ability to work with the agency and share problems
34. the foster family works through problems to a conclusion
    With respect to communication and problem-solving skills . . .
35. the foster family has a spiritual orientation toward handling problems
36. the foster mother's and father's determination to succeed as foster parents is high
37. the foster family's executive capacity is good
38. the foster family's ability to communicate under stress is good
39. the foster family's ability to share feelings is good
    With respect to handling stress . . .
40. the foster family's stress tolerance is high
41. the foster family's ability to handle anger is good
42. the foster family has had experience with death and grief
    With respect to its own extended family and the foster child's own family . . .
43. the foster family's relationship to its own extended family is good
44. the foster family maintains generational boundaries
45. the foster family can tolerate the child's own family
    A motivating and/or precipitating factor in taking a foster child into the home was . . .
46. having a specific child in mind
47. contact with other foster parents
48. being good friends with other foster families
49. inability to adopt
50. being approached by the agency
51. being "Casey long-term"
52. a large change or changes in the family situation
53. a physical change in the home such as a vacant bedroom
54. having time and love now that their own children were grown
55. need of a playmate for an own child
56. a desire for a second chance to be a better parent and/or guilt regarding their own children
57. attainment of financial security
58. liking children and/or a feeling of closeness to young people
59. a need to be a parent to any and all children
60. social commitment, as to a better world or to do something useful
    Specific characteristics, that is, the foster family . . .
61. had previous experience with foster care
62. can tolerate unassimilated aspects of the foster child, such as symbolic retention of the biological parents
63. manifests an overnurturing or smothering climate in the foster home
64. exhibits competition between the foster mother and foster father for the child's affection
65. is child-centered

TABLE 8—Continued

66. has a formal religious commitment
67. exhibits a history of compulsive behavior in either or both foster parents
68. lives in a geographic location (in the state) similar to that of the biological family
69. is located in an urban, suburban, or rural setting
70. has a great tendency to move from one household or location to another
71. has an upper-, middle-, or lower-class social and economic lifestyle
    Foster parents' overall attitude toward the child is . . .
72. accepting and positive
73. parental rather than custodial
    Foster parents describe their overall relationship with the child as . . .
74. involving some problems
75. involving major problems

mother, what kind of role model she provided, and whether she had initiated taking the foster child into the home. Special attention was paid to women who had adopted an earth mother personal style. Several such overwhelmingly loving, accepting, caring, affectionate mothers were dominant figures in successful foster families in the Montana Division, and we wanted to see if the style itself would predict placement stability. We also asked whether foster mothers who were in the process of liberation were more or less likely to be associated with stable placements.

Whether the foster father was emotionally involved with the child appeared to be an important determiner of placement success, including also how strong a masculine role model the foster father provided, whether it was he who had initiated taking on a foster child, and whether he was in the process of mid-life reassessment.

How the foster child fits into the age structure of the children of the foster parents is a matter that child welfare professionals have hypothesized to be related to placement success. Number of foster parents' children living at home is another such factor, as are the presence of foster parents' preschool children who might have kept their parents attuned to the needs of a high-maintenance group, and whether the foster family had experience with the age group of the foster child.

Several aspects of the marriage of the foster parents were used as predictors of placement stability: length of their marriage, since we thought older foster parents were more likely to be successful; whether they had been married previously; their actual commitment to child-rearing; and/or whether taking the foster child was an attempt to avoid starting a new phase of marriage. We also asked whether the foster parents were comfortable in their several roles within the family, whether they seemed at ease with one another, and whether they encouraged a physically affectionate family style.

Problem-solving and communication skills have been a hallmark of successful foster families in the Montana Division, especially the ability to work with the agency, to share problems and feelings, and to work problems through to a conclusion. Along this line is the motivation factor: some foster parents seemed much more determined to succeed than others. Several strong families, and a couple of weaker ones, exhibited a spiritual orientation toward problem solving, and we decided to see whether, overall, it was a predictor of more or less positive results.

Organizational, managerial ability is something usually thought of in connection with businesses and corporations rather than families, but several Montana Division families were notable in this respect, which we labeled "executive capacity," and saw as a possible influence on placement maintenance.

The ability to handle stress, and especially to communicate while under stress, is very important to the foster parents of especially disadvantaged children and so it was explored, in addition to the foster family's ability to handle anger and its experience with death and grief.

Many Casey families in the Montana Division appeared to have forged exceptionally good relationships with their extended families, often by setting and maintaining generational boundaries. This variable was viewed as a possible structural determinant of placement success, as was the ability of the foster family to tolerate, or accept, the child's biological family.

The factors that motivate a family to take on a foster child or that precipitate its acceptance into their home may be presumed to be powerful indicators of their ultimate success or failure with the child, and we took note of 15 that had occurred with some frequency in the Montana Division.

Having a specific child in mind was the first factor. Finding a specific individual an attractive addition to one's family seemed to denote the possibility of especially strong bonding. The desire to adopt but being unable to (for any of a variety of reasons) also seemed to bespeak the possibility of an unusual degree of motivation to succeed as foster parents.

Having continued contact with another couple (or couples) who are foster parents, or being close friends with another such couple (or couples) was viewed as likely to provide a powerful model for prospective foster parents.

The agency itself, of course, seeks out families that have the potential to be good foster parents and uses to good advantage its "Casey long-term" families, those that have served well in the past. We looked into the degree to which these variables were predictors of placement maintenance.

Certain changes in the family situation seemed possible indicators of success, including having time and love for another child once the foster family's own children were grown; physical factors in the home, such as having had a bedroom become vacant; having attained a hoped-for degree of financial security; or the need for a playmate for a child of the foster family following a move or the leaving home of older brothers and sisters.

Parents looking for a second chance to do a good job or for the opportunity to alleviate guilt about their behavior toward their own children sometimes have been selected as foster parents, and the Montana Division wanted to determine whether these motivations were more closely related to placement maintenance or placement breakdown.

Some rather general but presumably positive attitudes that characterized some successful foster parents were a feeling of closeness to children and young people, a need to be a parent to any and all children, and straightforward social commitment to a better world through better cared-for children.

Some fairly specific factors that the Montana Division had taken into account in choosing foster families and which it wished to evaluate with respect to placement stability were whether the family had had previous experience with foster care; whether it appeared able to tolerate the unassimilated aspects of the foster child; whether it was child-centered; whether it had a formal religious commitment; whether it lived in a geographic location in the state similar to that of the biological family; whether it dwelt in a rural, urban, or suburban setting; whether it had a greater than usual tendency to move from one household or location to another; and its social and economic lifestyle.

Two possible negative factors we examined were the presence of an overnurturing or smothering climate in the foster home, and a background of compulsive behavior in one or both foster parents.

As additional variables that might relate to placement maintenance, we asked whether the overall attitudes of foster parents to the child were primarily parental rather than custodial, and accepting and positive rather than neutral or negative. We also asked whether the foster parents described the situation as involving "some" problems, or "major" problems. Here our interest was directed to whether the perceived *and stated* magnitude of difficulties involving the child was related to placement maintenance.

Domain IX   Factors Involved in Placement Breakdown
While in TCFP

Domain IX includes factors involved in, or associated with, or responsible for, placement breakdown or change while the child was

DEAN

Dean is a young man of 18. He cultivates an unreactive, and in fact slightly subnormal, expression with those he doesn't know or trust, but he is of above-normal intelligence and very perceptive.

Dean's parents had created such a disruptive, frightening, and abusive environment that by the time he was five he was thought to be deaf and slightly retarded because he was so unreactive. He was taken from the home by state welfare officials, who placed him in a series of foster homes. In each case, the placement broke down because of Dean's almost total unresponsiveness. At the age of six, he was taken on by The Casey Family Program and placed with his present family. In trying to understand Dean's problems, his foster parents attended every seminar offered by TCFP that they could get to, read all the material given them, and consulted with the caseworker almost constantly at first. They made a dedicated commitment to do whatever they could to help Dean.

In the case of Dean's foster mother, this was partly due to the fact that she is an energetic if somewhat irascible woman who does throw herself into whatever she is doing, but it was partly due to her feeling that she had not quite succeeded with her four own children. They were the product of a marriage previous to the current one in which Dean is being raised. She had to work to support the children when the marriage broke up, and two of the four seem unable to make a reasonable, responsible adult life.

All four of the adult children feel both a closeness to Dean and resentment of him. They regard him as a real younger brother, but a privileged one: their mother has stayed home with him, as she was not able to do with them; there are more resources for him, both because of TCFP money and also their stepfather's job. And there is a suspicion on their part that somehow they weren't "enough" for their mother. Dean's foster mother, however, feels that she is a better mother to all her children, including Dean, and that the family as a whole is functioning better because of what she learned in trying to help Dean.

Dean's foster father has no children of his own. He is a rather quiet but warm and strong man. He has simply made Dean his son.

Dean has become an exceptionally healthy person over the last 12 years. He is doing well academically, he is active in athletics, he intends to go to college, and he knows that he has his family behind him.

enrolled in The Casey Family Program. These items apply only to the children who had suffered a placement breakdown or change while in the Program (Table 9). They are not, of course, intended as predictors and will be used to describe the circumstances of placement breakdown.

Although many factors had been observed to be involved in placement breakdowns, many of them seemed to be *ex post facto* descriptions of a particular situation rather than statements with general validity. Thus, we decided to retrieve information about each child and each foster family *for whom a breakdown had occurred* on each postulated breakdown factor and see which variables seemed most generally related to placement breakdown or change.

We looked first at what seemed to be purposeful attempts to end the fostering relationship—by the child or by the family, at the "gradual" and the "sudden" development of friction between child and family, and the family's losing its motivation to keep the child. We evaluated the possibility of an initial mismatch between the child and the family, also taking into account the breakdown, by divorce or desertion, for example, of the foster family.

We examined three child-related factors: showing stress in the placement setting long after the placement occurred, exhibiting anniversary effects, and retaining the biological parents in symbolic form.

Finally, we considered the possibility that the child had developed beyond the limits of the foster family to care for it. Here, obviously, development due to nurturing or emancipation was excluded.

Domain X   Caseworker's Professional Orientation

Domain X lists the professional orientations of the caseworkers in the Montana Division of The Casey Family Program in early 1980, as they described themselves. Although it did not appear on the surface that professional orientation was related to placement breakdown or change, we decided to examine systematically its effects as a potential predictor. Descriptive terms are listed in Table 10. It should be noted that the orientations are not mutually exclusive and that caseworkers typically described themselves with two of the terms.

Outcome Measures

The primary outcome measure in the first study was the number of placement breakdowns or changes that had occurred while the foster child

TABLE 9

Domain IX   Factors Involved in Placement Breakdown (PB)

Item

A *factor involved in placement breakdown or change is* . . .

1. the sudden development of friction between the child and the foster family
2. the gradual development of friction between the child and the foster family
3. purposeful initiation of the breakdown by the child
4. purposeful initiation of the breakdown by the foster family
5. an initial mismatch between the child and the foster family
6. breakdown (e.g., divorce, desertion) of the foster family
7. the foster family lost its motivation to keep the child
8. the foster child showed stress in the placement setting long after the placement occurred
9. the foster child exhibited, and continued to exhibit over several years, anniversary effects
10. retention in symbolic form by the foster child of his or her parents
11. development or maturation of the child beyond the limits of the foster family (excluding development due to nurturing or emancipation)

was in care with TCFP. "Placement breakdown or change" denotes a situation in which, either de facto as in a runaway, or in the judgment of the professional staff of the Montana Division, a child had to be transferred from the care of one foster family to another or, temporarily, to some other form of care.

Although placement maintenance seemed to be a primary indicator of successful foster care and one strongly related to emancipation into productive adult life, it is not without fault as a measure of placement success, and it is not the only possible measure. That is, some placements are maintained that are far from optimal for either foster child or foster family. Some placements, albeit few, endure for years in the face of stress and strife. Therefore, we used two other measures of placement success. The first of these was a rating (on a nine-point scale), by the caseworker responsible for a given child, of the present, overall global level of functioning of the child; the second was a similar rating of the functioning of the foster family. The assumption underlying this second rating was that, other factors being more or less equal, better placements would be associated with foster families that functioned more effectively.

In addition, we studied the relationships of our predictor variables with what we considered a secondary outcome measure, the willingness (on a five-point scale) of the caseworker to place a child, not necessarily the same one, with the foster family if the choice were to be made again

TABLE 10

Domain X   Caseworker's Professional Orientation (PO)

Item

Caseworker describes his or her professional orientation or style as . . .
1. supportive
2. client-oriented
3. family-oriented
4. confronting

on the basis of present knowledge. In our discussions, willingness appeared to be an interesting amalgam of the three primary outcome measures.

Finally, we studied the relationships of our predictors to two other variables: the child's age upon entering TCFP, and the total number of placements the child had had before entering TCFP. We were interested in the former instance in factors that might put children at relatively younger or older ages into the dire straits typical of most children TCFP takes on. In the latter case we hoped to be able to point to variables, especially those involving risk factors, that made foster children vulnerable to repeated placement breakdown in situations outside the supportive structure of TCFP.

The outcome variables are listed in Tables 11 and 12.

The pattern of relationships among the primary predictors and between the primary predictors and the secondary predictor will be discussed when we consider the results of the first study.

TABLE 11

Primary Outcome Variables (OVP)

Item	Scale
1. Number of placement breakdowns or changes while in TCFP	Number*
2. Caseworker's rating of the present, overall global level of functioning of the foster child	1–9**
3. Caseworker's rating of the present, overall global level of functioning of the foster family	1–9**

*Always 0, 1, or 2 for the 51 children in this sample

**1 = extremely poor functioning; 5 = functioning neither good nor bad; 9 = extremely good functioning

TABLE 12

Secondary and Related Outcome Variables (OVS)

Item	Scale
1. Caseworker's willingness to place a foster child with the same foster family if the choice were to be made again on the basis of present knowledge	− 2 to + 2*
2. Child's age upon entering TCFP	Years
3. Number of placements the child had before entering TCFP	Number

*To be described in Chapter 3

3

Study I   Technical Considerations

In this chapter we consider technical matters associated with the data and their relation to the statistical techniques employed in the study; matters of response scales and reliability; frame of reference and halo effects; and the manner in which the data were edited, recorded, and verified for computer analysis.

Much of the information in the domains described in Chapter 2 represents material that is factual in the historical sense. The information in Domains I, VIII, and IX consists almost exclusively of ratings by caseworkers.

Domains III and V consist of judgments made by Margaret Stuart about the children in the sample, based upon available archival data, consultation with caseworkers, and her professional experience.

It should be noted that there is an occasional factual item in some domains consisting primarily of ratings, and vice versa. The remarks that follow pertain to item types, that is, factual or rating/judgmental, rather than to a domain as a whole.

Response Scales and Reliability

The factual information in the case files had been carefully researched by Montana Division caseworkers and other staff members, often reconfirming the findings of various social agencies and/or the courts. Where facts were in doubt or the authenticity of information was in question, the case files stated that this was indeed the situation.

To test the data further, an exhaustive search for inconsistencies was made by means of computerized cross-tabulations. For example, a child with no siblings should not have been recorded as exhibiting competition with a sibling or having been in recent contact with one or more siblings. Based on the frequency of inconsistencies, the factual data in the case files were 97 to 98 percent accurate.

Each caseworker retrieved the factual information from case files on the foster children under his or her supervision. Where an item provided a correct description of a child, the worker recorded a "1" on the data sheet. If the item did not correctly describe the child, a "0" was recorded. Wherever the authenticity of an item was in doubt, no response was recorded, and the response to the item for that child was excluded from descriptive summaries and statistical analyses. Variables such as "number of placements before being accepted into TCFP" and "number of biological siblings" were recorded simply as the appropriate cardinal number.

Margaret Stuart's judgments of characteristic responses to threat and serious risk factors in the child's history were made on a present/absent basis. If a response to threat or a risk factor was judged to be present, a "1" was recorded, whereas a "0" signified its absence. If the issue was in doubt, nothing was recorded, and the response to the item for that child was excluded from descriptive summaries and statistical analyses.

To provide an estimate of the reliability of her judgments, Stuart reworked her summaries for four children after a lapse of eight months. The index of agreement between the first and second ratings was .96. It was calculated as the number of individual items agreed upon, that is, a "1" on both occasions or a "0" on both occasions, divided by the total number of items (over the four summaries) rated.

Although this procedure provides considerable assurance of the stability of Stuart's ratings, it leaves open the question of inter-rater reliability, that is, the extent to which her judgments might have differed from those of another equally informed and experienced professional. Unfortunately, we have no data that speak directly to this question. Stuart's credentials and experience, however, argue for a substantial degree of objectivity and accuracy.

Assessments of personal characteristics of the foster child, characteristics of the present foster family, and factors involved in placement breakdown while in TCFP were, with the exception of factual items (e.g., "foster mother works outside the home"), based on caseworkers' ratings on a scale that ran from -2 to $+2$.

Caseworkers used a "1" to indicate that an item was, in their judgment, an appropriate description. A " − 1" signified that it was an inappropriate description. If the caseworker was uncertain whether the item did or did not describe a child, a "0" was recorded. Where an item was especially descriptive of a child, a "2" was used to indicate it; a " − 2" signified that an item was an especially poor description of a child. Caseworkers were discouraged from using "2" and " − 2" ratings unless extreme instances made them obviously appropriate.

Practice items were used in two group rating sessions to make sure that the use of the scale, and especially of the uncertain (0) and extreme (2, − 2) categories, was understood by all and that acceptable inter-rater reliability had been achieved in rating three sets of five children known to all of them. The children in the last set of five were currently enrolled in TCFP. The four caseworkers involved achieved a level of agreement on 20 items (over the last five children) in the second practice session that ranged from .88 for the lowest pair of raters to 1.00 for the two highest pairs (there were six pairings among the four raters).[a] The agreement index was calculated as the number of items agreed upon divided by the total number of items rated. An agreement involved having both members of a pair of raters use *exactly the same rating* from among the five permitted (− 2, − 1, 0, 1, 2).

Global ratings of the overall functioning of the foster child and foster family and of the caseworker's willingness to choose a foster family were again also practiced until a level of agreement between every pair of raters of at least .90 was achieved.

It might be noted that more sophisticated indices of inter-rater agreement, such as Cohen's kappa, could have been employed, but, given the high levels of agreement achieved, their values would have been similar. Moreover, the inferential possibilities they provide, either in distinguishing results from chance or calculating confidence intervals, are not of great importance with levels of agreement among raters as high as those achieved in this study.

Frame of Reference and Halo Phenomena

Frame of reference effects can be a problem with ratings on five-point Likert scales such as the ones used here. That is, if one were to rate a sample of children on an item where the ratings tended to be generally

---

[a] Although potentially troublesome items were selected for the practice sessions, the inter-rater reliability over items not tested may of course have been less than over those examined.

low, the frame of reference to give low ratings could carry over to ratings on another item where low ratings were not appropriate. Or if one were to rate each child on all items, a series of low ratings might precede an item on which a low rating was not appropriate and cause it to be rated too low. To minimize such problems, caseworkers were instructed to rate a single item at a time for all children under their supervision and to reconsider routinely the first half-dozen ratings on that item before going on to the next item.

Halo phenomena can also be a problem with ratings of variables such as personal characteristics. Differential attractiveness or visibility among a set of children can, especially among peers rating each other, lead to similar ratings on items that are intended to tap distinct factors. Caseworkers were sensitized to this problem before making their ratings and urged to refer their judgments to specific behavioral characteristics, where possible, to avoid this pitfall.

To check for such halo effects, Pearson correlation coefficients were computed for all pairs of personal characteristics before proceeding with the main analysis. The average correlation for these pairs of variables was .24. Only eight pairs of rated variables had correlations greater than .35, and only three of these were greater than .45. It was concluded that halo effects did not constitute a problem in this study.

Data Editing, Recording, and Verification

The data sheets from the four Montana Division caseworkers were edited before being recorded. They were first inspected for missing data that the overall pattern of responses for a given child suggested should be present. Seemingly contradictory responses were noted. Ratings with opposite signs that appeared to be inconsistent were recorded, and all of these matters, an average of about a dozen, were brought to the attention of each caseworker and verified or corrected.

The edited responses were then punched into computer disk files and printouts generated. The printouts were proofed by traditional text comparison procedures and corrections made. Cross-tabulations and histograms were then constructed by means of computer routines to pinpoint remaining inconsistencies, outliers, and errors. The final corrected data file was then subjected to tabulation procedures and statistical analysis.

4

Descriptive Summary of the Children of the Montana Division

Before discussing the factors that predicted placement maintenance and the other outcome measures, we devote a few pages to describing the foster children of the Montana Division. Although the vignettes speak to the background and situation of individual children, it helps also to provide a sense of the characteristics that distinguish the foster children under the care of The Casey Family Program in Montana as a group, to describe the foster families of the Montana Division in terms of their important characteristics, to examine factors that led to placement breakdown and to look into the caseworkers' professional orientations.

Domain I   Personal Characteristics of the Foster Child

Five of the items in Domain I characterize the group to a substantial degree. The children were rated by their caseworkers as likeable, physically attractive, and neatly dressed and groomed. They were seen as tending to be afraid of intimacy, but they were not viewed as being unique. That is, their problems, background, and present situation were far from ordinary, but had not transformed them into children who were in any basic way unlike others.

Twenty-nine percent of the children had a hobby to which they were seriously devoted. The only relatively common hobbies were music and athletics.

Domain II   Demographic Characteristics of the Foster Child

Fifty-nine percent of the children were males and 41 percent were females. Their average age was almost exactly 14 years. Sixteen percent of them were six to ten years old, 49 percent were 11 to 15, and 35 percent were from 16 to 22.

In terms of racial background, 63 percent of the sample were identified as Caucasian, 6 percent were Native American, 18 percent were mixed Native American and other race(s), and 13 percent belonged to other races, other racial combinations, or were of unknown racial background.

Twenty-six percent of the children were identified as Catholic, 6 percent were Mormons, 16 percent were affiliated with various Protestant denominations, and 52 percent were either members of non-Christian faiths or, most often, did not have a religious affiliation.

Domain III   The Foster Child's Characteristic Responses to Threat

Although a great variety of responses to threat occurred in individual children, only four types of responses characterized 10 percent or more of them. In order of descending frequency they were passive-aggressive behavior—39 percent; aggression or violence—25 percent; acting out—18 percent; and withdrawn or moody behavior—14 percent.

In addition to being the most common response to threat, passive-aggressive behavior was by far the most negatively responded to by caseworkers and foster parents alike. Violence and aggression and the more dramatic forms of acting out attracted immediate attention and decisive action, but it was the passive-aggressive style in a foster child that labeled him or her as difficult to deal with and having a poor prognosis for placement maintenance.

Domain IV   History of the Biological Family

Both parents were known for 77 percent of the children, 41 percent of the children's parents were divorced, and, in 28 percent of the cases, one or both parents were known to be deceased.

For mothers for whom data were available, average age at the birth of the foster child was 24 years and four months, but 39 percent were 22 years of age or younger.

In 69 percent of the cases, the current location of the mother was known, and, in 51 percent of these cases, it was in Montana. The mother had some contact with her child in 41 percent of the cases, had no contact or involvement 29 percent of the time, and was known to be hospitalized or institutionalized in 25 percent of the instances.

Forty-one percent of the mothers of the foster children had rejected, abused, neglected, or deserted them, and 45 percent had a history of alcohol problems, mental illness, or suicide attempts. In 20 percent of the case files, it was noted that the mother had been very attached to or very affectionate with her child.

The current location of 43 percent of the fathers was known, and in 24 percent of these instances, it was in Montana.

The average age of the father at the birth of the foster child was, when data were available, 30 years and four months.

The father had regular or sporadic contact with the child in 16 percent of cases, no contact in 57 percent of cases, and 27 percent of the time no information was available.

Sixteen percent of the fathers had a history of alcohol problems, 12 percent had a criminal record, and about 4 percent were hospitalized with chronic health problems.

Thirty-one percent of the fathers had rejected the child or failed to accept or had no relationship with him or her. Four percent were known to have abused the child.

Ninety percent of the children had half- or full-siblings, and 88 percent of the time one or more of the siblings was within five years of the child's own age. Every third child had a sibling who was also served by TCFP, and one in 12 had more than one.

In one case in five, there was little or no information available regarding past relationships with siblings, but 76 percent of the children in the sample who had siblings were known to have lived with one or more of them in the past, and 35 percent had had a close relationship with at least one sibling; however, 30 percent of the children with siblings had had a poor relationship or active rivalry with one or more of their siblings.

With respect to present relationships with siblings, 28 percent of the children had frequent contact with siblings, 39 percent had sporadic contact, 26 percent had no present contact, and in 7 percent of the instances, little or no such information existed.

Fifty-three percent of the children were reported to have no relatives other than parents or siblings who had been important figures in their past; however, 60 percent had relatives who at present played an important role in their lives or with whom they were in meaningful contact.

A third of the time, relatives who had been important in the past were grandparents. A sixth of the time, the important relative was an aunt, uncle, or cousin.

Domain V   Serious Risk Factors in the Foster Child's History

Nine factors thought to put the foster child seriously at risk were present in the histories of at least 10 percent of the children. In order of descending frequency of occurrence, these were rejection by mother—39 percent; failure of early foster placements—39 percent; physical or emotional abuse—37 percent; alcohol problems in the family—31 percent; mother's illness, death, or suicide—29 percent; neglect—29 percent; family turmoil or disruption—26 percent; desertion by father—20 percent; and divorce—20 percent.

Domain VI   Placement History

Forty-one percent of the children had been in foster placements before their current one. The average age at first placement was six years and six weeks, but for half of the children it had taken place before they reached their sixth birthdays. For three-eighths of the children, it occurred between six and ten years of age, and, for the last one-eighth, at age 11 or later.

The most common setting for a first placement outside the home was foster care—it accounted for 49 percent of the initial placements. Next most common was a placement with friends or relatives—28 percent, followed by a receiving home—14 percent, and an institution—6 percent.

Six reasons for first placement were cited in 10 percent or more of cases. In order of descending frequency, they were some combination of desertion, abuse, relinquishment, or family disruption—53 percent; death or health problem of parent(s)—29 percent; relinquishment alone—

26 percent; abuse and neglect of child—24 percent; health of parent(s) alone—22 percent; and behavior problems of child—10 percent.

Among children in the sample who had placements subsequent to the first one, the average number was five. Sixty-eight percent had 0–5 subsequent placements, 24 percent had 6–10 subsequent placements; 6 percent had 11–15 subsequent placements, and 2 percent had more than 15. Almost a third of the children had at least one placement in an institution.

The most common child-related category of reasons for placement breakdown before admission to TCFP was violent or aggressive behavior by itself or in conjunction with acting out that involved drinking, stealing, sexual behavior, or firesetting. These behaviors were cited in 31 percent of the cases. Nine other child-related categories of reasons for placement breakdown were mentioned. In order of descending frequency, they were untrustworthiness—16 percent; passive-aggressive behavior—16 percent; hyperactivity—12 percent; anger, hostility, and withdrawal—8 percent; failure to integrate into the foster family—8 percent; inability to cope with authority—8 percent; inability of the foster parent(s) to cope with the child—6 percent; running away—6 percent; and tantrums—4 percent.

Among the risk factors cited as involved with breakdown of subsequent placements before TCFP placement, seven occurred in more than 10 percent of instances. In order of decreasing frequency, they were school problems—43 percent; the nature of the placement itself—29 percent; rejection by the foster family—18 percent; foster family disruption—18 percent; death of a parent or foster parent—16 percent; peer problems—12 percent; and acting out—12 percent.

In 14 percent of cases there were instances in which a stepfather was abusive, but in 14 percent of cases past adoptive parents became significant supportive figures to the children. In 10 percent of cases, continuing contact with past foster parents was noted as occurring.

Relinquishment by the parents had occurred for 75 percent of the foster children. On the average, it had taken place almost exactly six years previously, but the time period ranged from one month to more than 12 years.

Domain VII   Present Placement Situation

Of the 51 children in the sample, 39 were in long-term family care, four were in quasi-independent care, two were in a public institution, two were in the Scholarship Program, two were in a group home setting, one was in private residential care, and the whereabouts of the other child were unknown.

Forty-two percent of the children in the sample were located in the Helena area near the Montana Division's headquarters, 24 percent were in the Great Falls area, 16 percent were in the Missoula area, and 16 percent lived elsewhere in Montana, chiefly in rural settings. Fifty-three percent of the children from minority group backgrounds were placed in corresponding minority homes.

The average age of the children upon entering TCFP was ten years and nine months. Forty-three percent had been accepted by 1975 or before, 28 percent had been accepted in 1976 or 1977, and 29 percent were accepted in 1978 or later. In 53 percent of the cases, the Montana Division had contact with the biological mother, and in 45 percent it had some contact with the biological father.

In their placement, 14 percent of the children had continuing contacts with their mother, and 29 percent were in sporadic contact. Six percent had continuing contacts with their father and eight percent were in sporadic contact.

The Foster Child: A Composite Picture

Before discussing the characteristics of the foster families, we will sketch a composite portrait of the typical foster child under care in the Montana Division.

The modal child was a 14-year-old white male with no formal religious affiliation. He was physically attractive, dressed and groomed himself neatly, and was inclined to avoid relationships that required closeness or intimacy. His characteristic responses to threat were acting out and passive-aggressive behavior.

The child's parents were known, were living, and were about equally likely still to be married to each other or to be divorced. The mother was slightly more than 24 years old when the foster child was born. Her present location was known, and it was equally as likely to be in Montana as out of state. She had no present contact with her child. The father was 30 years old when his child was born, his current location was unknown, and he had no contact with his child.

The child had one or more siblings, at least one of whom was within five years of his own age, had lived with one or more of them at some time in the past, and was in present contact with one or more of them. His relatives, other than parents or siblings, had not been important to him in the past, but he was presently in contact with one or more of them.

The child's first placement occurred at the age of six. It was necessitated by some combination of desertion, abuse, relinquishment, or family

JOHN

John is a small but strong-looking 11-year-old. He generally maintains a bland expression behind his glasses. He has been with his current Casey foster family for three years, and seems fairly comfortable with them.

John lived with his mother for the first six years of his life. She held fundamentalist Christian beliefs but also had bouts of heavy drinking and, in at least the last two years that John lived with her, engaged in prostitution. His father left the family when John was about two years old, and his whereabouts are unknown.

John was removed from his mother's custody by state welfare officials when he was six. He was placed by the state in a receiving home and then in a foster home. He ran away from both and then came to the attention of The Casey Family Program. After an extensive workup, including psychological testing, he was placed with a Casey family that had no particular religious leanings, because his mother's beliefs had created such conflict in John. He again ran away, however.

The Montana Division decided to try placing John in a very religious home, where such matters were given a great deal of weight, time, and discussion. This family had two children, one four years and one six years younger than he. The father had had a rough childhood and rather wild adolescence. He turned to religion in his late twenties. He is a man with a warm manner, often clasping John around the shoulders and giving him a hug, and though John doesn't seem to seek out such affection, he places himself so that it can occur. The foster mother is active with the church, but spends most of her time at home, keeping all three children constructively busy. John particularly requires this attention since he is inclined to shirk any work that he can and will disappear for hours, given the chance. He is not a child who makes friends easily, but he has a couple of neighborhood friends his own age, and several more who tolerate him unless his considerable temper gets out of control.

John has regained contact with his mother and receives about one phone call a week from her. He seems to be able to handle this without regressing, though he does tend to do so around the time of year when he was first removed from his mother.

John is doing adequately in school, has been accepted in his foster family as their son, which is indeed what they call him, and, though he still regards his mother as "his," wants to remain with his foster family.

disruption. The factors most likely to have put the child at risk were rejection by his mother, failure of early foster placements, and physical or emotional abuse.

Relinquishment by the parents had occurred six years ago, and the child's present placement was in long-term foster care. He lived in or near one of Montana's larger cities, and, if from a minority background, was placed in a minority home.

The child was nearly 11 years old when he entered The Casey Family Program, and his mother was in contact with the agency.

Domain VIII　　Characteristics of the Present Foster Family

We now present a sketch of the foster families of the Montana Division in terms of modal characteristics and average features. We begin with the foster mother and foster father as individuals and then discuss matters of family structure, style, and interaction.

Foster mothers averaged 42 years of age, were most frequently oldest children themselves, and had not graduated from high school. Most mothers did not work outside the home, and, where they did, enjoyed only modest job security. They were not in the process of liberation, and they provided a strong female role model in the foster family. The emotional coherence of the foster mother was not notably strong, however, on the average, and her style was not that of the earth mother. She was generally the parent who initiated taking a foster child into the home.

Foster fathers averaged 44 years of age, were most frequently oldest children themselves, and had not graduated from high school. The foster father was employed outside the home and had a reasonable degree of job security. He was not in the process of mid-life reassessment and provided a moderately strong male role model for the family, although not as much so as the female role model provided by his wife. He was strongly emotionally involved with the foster child, but was not the parent who had initiated taking on a foster child.

The foster parents had been married an average of 19 years and had not been married previously. There was a modest tendency for them to have made a commitment to child-rearing early in their marriage. Taking the foster child into their home was not seen as a new phase of child-rearing, nor was it by any means an attempt to avoid starting a new phase of marriage. The personal interaction of the foster mother and foster father was marked by a modest degree of ease and comfort in their several roles, but the family style did not stress physical affection.

The foster child tended to be younger than the own children in the foster family, but nearly as often was intermediate in age to the own children or was older than they. There were an average of two own children in the home but no preschoolers, and the foster family had had experience with the age group of the foster child.

The foster family had better than average ability to work with the agency and share problems and also to see through problems to a conclusion, but it did not have a spiritual orientation toward handling problems. The foster mother's and foster father's determination to succeed as foster parents was high. Their executive capacity was reasonably good, although their ability to communicate under stress was somewhat less so, and their capacity for sharing feelings was only average.

The overall tolerance for stress of the foster family was fairly adequate, as was its ability to handle anger. Its experience with death and grief was average; that is, like that of most families.

The foster family's relationship to its own extended family was strong, and it did a workmanlike job both of maintaining generational boundaries within its own extended family and of tolerating the biological family of the foster child.

With respect to motivating and/or precipitating factors for taking a foster child into the home, having a specific child in mind was not a factor, and, in fact, only being a "Casey long-term" or having a commitment to a better world appeared to be motivating factors of any strength.

In terms of specific characteristics, the foster family had not had previous experience with foster care, but found itself to have considerable ability to tolerate unassimilated aspects of the foster child, such as symbolic retention of the biological parents. There was a moderate tendency for the foster home to be child-centered and for a smothering, overnurturing climate to exist in it. The foster family did not have a formal religious commitment. There was not a background of compulsive behavior in either foster parent.

The foster family lived in a suburban area in a location unrelated to where in the state the biological parents resided, had very little tendency to move from one location to another, and enjoyed a middle-class lifestyle.

The foster parents' overall attitude toward the child was accepting and positive, but not parental. They described themselves as having no problems of any magnitude with the child.

Domain IX   Factors Involved in Placement Breakdown
While in TCFP

Twenty-seven percent, or 14 of 51, of the children in the sample had experienced a placement breakdown or change while in the Program. All had been in long-term family care, and, at the time of this study, five of the 14 were in a second foster home placement, five were in institutional settings, two had left the Program to begin independent living, and two had left for other or unknown reasons. Of the four young people who left the Program, the average age at termination was 17.

Of the 14 children who had experienced a placement breakdown or change, there were 12 cases where gradual reciprocal friction had developed between the child and his or her foster family, and there were two cases where sudden reciprocal friction developed. It appeared that in eight cases the child initiated the breakdown, whereas the foster family initiated it in six cases. In seven cases, the foster family appeared to have lost its motivation to keep the child, and in another the foster parents were divorced and the family was disrupted.

In the judgment of the caseworkers, a mismatch had been made between the child and the foster family in six instances, and in two others the foster child had developed beyond the foster family (not because of nurturing or emancipation). Ten children had shown stress in the foster home long after the original placement, and three exhibited anniversary effects. Eleven of the 14 children retained feelings of possession of the biological parents and/or a strong image of them.

Domain X   Caseworker's Professional Orientation

Finally, let us examine the professional orientations of the caseworkers of the Montana Division. Although each worker saw himself or herself as primarily supportive in orientation, each one modified that approach in terms of the foster child and foster family being served. In 40 percent of cases the worker was more family-oriented, in 40 percent of cases he or she was more client-oriented, in 10 percent of cases a confronting style was employed, and in 10 percent of cases nothing was added to the basic supportive approach.

5

Study I   Prediction of Outcomes

The major goal of the first study was the construction of statistical models for the prediction of the outcome variables, in particular, placement maintenance while enrolled in TCFP. In a rigorous sense, the models are postdictive, in that archival data retrieved from case files, assessments from Stuart's work, and caseworkers' ratings were used as pointers to placement breakdowns or changes that had already occurred. Although there is no logical difficulty with such an approach, its validity for actual predictive, that is, prospective, use remains in question until it is actually used to point to future placement breakdown or change.

Placement breakdown or change is just the other face of placement maintenance. In quantifying this variable, we let "0" stand for no placement breakdowns, or maintenance. Then "1" stood for a single breakdown, and "2" stood for two breakdowns, the maximum that had occurred among the members of the present sample. We have spoken here, and for convenience will continue to speak, of predicting placement breakdown or change. But we actually predicted *number of placement breakdowns or changes*. We could have chosen to try to predict either *maintenance*, "0," or the occurrence of *one or more breakdowns*, "1," but we did not. We felt that allowing the outcome variable to go to the limit of its actual range and take the more extreme value of "2" as well might allow us to find predictors that would more accurately point to the children most prone to placement failure.

We have spoken of "placement breakdown *or change*." It has frequently been the practice of the Montana Division not to wait for an outright rupture in a foster placement that seemed obviously headed for failure. A change to a new foster home has sometimes been made to provide a greater chance for future stability. But both outright breakdowns and planned changes were classed as placement failures and assigned to the same category for the purpose of predicting outcomes.

We would ideally have liked to search through the entire 282 variables in our ten domains simultaneously to find the best set of predictors for each outcome variable. Computer storage limitations prevented our doing so. We were constrained to consider a maximum of no more than 50 predictors at a time. To deal with this limitation, work progressed in two stages.

In the first stage we searched for predictors that correlated substantially with a given outcome variable, because, in multiple regression, the correlation of a predictor with an outcome variable is a good indicator of its utility in a model. As a rule of thumb, we retained only predictors that correlated |.35| or more with an outcome variable. Such a correlation indicates that the predictor accounts for approximately 10 percent of the variance in the outcome. This slightly conservative value might be expected to screen out some predictors that had only a fortuitous rather than a systematic relationship with the outcome measure.

In the second stage, we used a particular approach to model building in multiple regression called the "stepdown" procedure.[6] (We would have preferred the sometimes more effective "stepwise" procedure, but the computer software to implement it was not available to us at that time.) In the stepdown procedure, the regression of all the independent variables considered as possible predictors of a given outcome variable is computed. Then the unique contribution of each predictor to the outcome variable is calculated and the one that contributes least to the prediction is tested. The test involves an analysis of whether the prediction of the outcome variable suffers in any substantial way if the variable being tested is dropped. If the prediction would suffer, that is, become materially less accurate, all variables being considered are retained and the prediction equation includes them all. But if the predictability of the outcome variable would not be altered materially by dropping the test variable, it is eliminated and another cycle begins.

In the second cycle, the regression of all of the remaining predictors on the outcome variable is computed, and the unique contribution of each independent variable is again calculated. The least effective independent variable in the second cycle is tested. If dropping this variable would not materially affect the predictability of the outcome variable, it is dropped, and a third cycle is begun.

The cycling continues until a set of independent variables remains, none of which could be dropped without significantly reducing the predictability of the outcome variable. An F-test is used as the criterion for dropping a variable in this procedure. Its value was set at 4.0 throughout the analyses described below, corresponding roughly to an alpha level of .05. This rather liberal value in a situation such as ours might ordinarily be expected to result in the retention of more predictor variables than would be optimal. We felt, however, that the first stage of the selection procedure had probably eliminated most of the marginally useful predictors and that the risk of including "noise" variables was small.

This two-stage approach had the disadvantage that it may have eliminated some variables with so-called "suppressor" effects, that is, which together with specific other predictors would have added to the predictability of the outcome variable by means of interaction effects. These effects are frequently subtle and of considerable interest, but we were unable to pursue them as completely as would have been desirable.

Statistical models were generated for each of the four outcome variables previously discussed. Each is described in a separate section below. Each section contains a table listing the variables that correlated |.35| or more with the outcome variable and the values of the correlations. All variables that correlated |.35| or higher with the outcome variable constituted the set of predictors considered in the first cycle of the stepdown procedure.

The second segment of each section provides a verbal description of the relationships listed in the table to clarify their interpretation. The statistical model, expressed here as a regression equation resulting from the stepdown procedure, is then presented, together with information about its accuracy and limitations.

Outcome: Placement Breakdown or Change

The variables that correlated |.35| or more with the occurrence of one or more placement breakdowns while in TCFP are listed in Table 13. Verbal statements of the relationships are given below. The strongest relationships between predictor variables and placement maintenance are stated first, followed by those that accounted for less variance.

It should be noted that for a binary variable, such as the first one discussed below, it is usual to speak not of the quantity of one variable increasing (for a positive correlation) or decreasing (for a negative correlation) with an increasing quantity of the other, but of the *probability* or *likelihood* of the binary variable increasing (for a positive correlation) or

TABLE 13

Predictor Variables That Correlated |.35| or More with Occurrence of One or More Placement Breakdowns While in TCFP

	Variable	Correlation
PH-24	Child had one or more placement(s) in institution(s).	.53
PF-25	With respect to their marriage, the foster parents have been married ——— years.	−.49
PF-62	The foster family can tolerate unassimilated aspects of the foster child, such as symbolic retention of the biological parents.	−.47
PH-29	Child-related reason for placement breakdown(s) before enrollment in TCFP was passive-aggressive behavior.	.46
PF-43	Foster family's relationship to its own extended family is good.	−.44
PH-41	Risk factor in placements outside the own home subsequent to the first was failure to attach.	.41
RT-8	Child's response to threat is running away.	.41
DC-2	Child is ——— years of age.	.40
PF-17	Foster father is emotionally involved with the child.	−.39
PF-63	The foster family manifests an overnurturing or smothering climate in the foster home.	−.37
PF-65	The foster home is child-centered.	−.37
PF-8	Foster mother possesses strong emotional coherence.	−.37
PH-18	Number of placements outside the own home (and before enrollment in TCFP) subsequent to the first is ———.	.37
PP-20	Child was accepted by the program when he or she was ——— years of age.	.36
PH-4	Child was 11 years of age or older at first placement.	.35
NF-18	Biological father currently has no contact and no involvement with the child.	−.35
PF-11	Foster father is ——— years of age.	−.35

decreasing (for a negative correlation) with an increasing quantity of the other.

Interpretation

PH-24.   The more likely it was that a child had one or more placement(s) in institution(s), the larger the number of placement breakdowns he or she had suffered while in TCFP.

PF-25. The longer the foster parents had been married, the smaller the number of placement breakdowns the child had suffered while in TCFP.

PF-62. The better the foster family was rated in ability to tolerate unassimilated aspects of the foster child, such as symbolic retention of the biological parents, the smaller the number of placement breakdowns he or she had suffered while in TCFP.

PH-29. The greater the likelihood that a child-related reason for placement breakdown before enrollment in TCFP was judged to be passive-aggressive behavior, the larger the number of placement breakdowns the child had suffered while in TCFP.

PF-43. The better the foster family's relationship to its own extended family was rated, the smaller the number of placement breakdowns the child had suffered while in TCFP.

PH-41. The greater the likelihood that a risk factor in placements outside the own home subsequent to the first was judged to be failure to attach, the larger the number of placement breakdowns the child had suffered while in TCFP.

RT-8. The greater the likelihood that a child's response to threat was running away, the larger the number of placement breakdowns he or she had suffered while in TCFP.

DC-2. The older the child, the larger the number of placement breakdowns he or she had suffered while in TCFP.

PF-17. The more the foster father was rated as emotionally involved with the child, the smaller the number of placement breakdowns the child had suffered while in TCFP.

PF-63. The more the foster family was rated as manifesting an overnurturing or smothering climate in the foster home, the smaller the number of placement breakdowns the child had suffered while in TCFP.

PF-65. The more the foster home was rated as child-centered, the smaller the number of placement breakdowns the child had suffered while in TCFP.

PF-8. The more the foster mother was rated as possessing strong emotional coherence, the smaller the number of placement breakdowns the child had suffered while in TCFP.

PH-18. The larger the number of placements a child had outside the own home (and before enrollment in TCFP) subsequent to the first, the larger the number of placement breakdowns he or she had suffered while in TCFP.

PP-20. The older the child at the time of acceptance into TCFP, the larger the number of placement breakdowns he or she had suffered while in TCFP.

PH-4.   The more likely that a child was 11 years of age or older at first placement, the larger the number of placement breakdowns he or she had suffered while in TCFP.

NF-18.   The more likely it was that the biological father had no current contact and no involvement with the child, the smaller the number of placement breakdowns the child had suffered while in TCFP.

PF-11.   The older the foster father, the smaller the number of placement breakdowns the child had suffered while in TCFP.

Of the 17 predictors that correlated l.35l or more with placement maintenance, eight of them involved the foster family. Foster parents who had been married longer and had maintained a good relationship with their own extended family were strongly associated with placement stability. It seems apparent that veteran foster parents who have functioned for years in their own extended family are more capable of maintaining a relationship with a deprived foster child of the kind TCFP specializes in. Experience does count and may be the primary factor that allows the foster family to tolerate unassimilated aspects of the child.

The emotional coherence of the foster mother was positively related to placement maintenance, and, together with a more mature foster father who is emotionally involved with the foster child, is probably what contributes most to a home that is child-centered.

It seems paradoxical that an overnurturing, or smothering, climate in the foster home was associated with stable placements. It is tempting to speculate that an emotionally deprived child might find a climate that would smother an ordinary young person to be exactly what he or she needs to maintain a feeling of being wanted and valued. Our data do not allow us to do more than speculate, but this finding is certainly one that invites further research.

The biological family hardly came into the picture except in the person of the father. His *lack* of contact and involvement with his child was associated with placement maintenance. Fathers have been known as upsetters of foster placements, and our findings offer support to this bit of lore.

The age of the foster child was strongly related to placement maintenance. An older child and one accepted into the program at a more advanced age—especially when 11 or older—was much more likely to be involved in a placement breakdown or change. Older children are also, of course, more likely to have had many foster placements, another predictor of breakdown or change.

Having had one or more placements in an institution was the single strongest predictor of placement breakdown. The reason for this well-known finding involves a chicken-and-egg problem. Does institutional life affect a child so negatively that he or she is forever unsuited to life in a family setting? Or are children who are unsuited to family life from the beginning more likely to be institutionalized?

Three more specifically child-related factors were all associated with placement breakdown or change: passive-aggressive behavior, failure to attach in earlier placements, and running away. Although it seems obvious that children who do not attach and those who run can rupture even the potentially strongest foster placements, passive-aggressive behavior seems a less clear-cut predictor of breakdown. Based on the statements of one caseworker after another and one foster parent after another, however, the passive-aggressive child may be one of nature's least loved creatures. The combination of alternating unreactivity and aggressive balkiness may be more trying of parental and professional patience and good will than any other. Even violence and violent acting out were more acceptable to most foster parents in terms of maintaining foster placements.

The Regression Equation

What is the prescription for placement maintenance given by these predictors? The (stepdown) regression equation states, by the variables it includes, which of our predictors are most important. "Important" has a slightly different meaning here than its usual one. We are looking for predictors that are important in that they contribute *independent* information about placement stability. Thus, a predictor, even the one most highly correlated with the outcome variable, may not wind up in the equation if the information it carries is also carried by one or more other variables that contribute additional unique input as well. For example, it appears that PH-24, "Child has had one or more placement(s) in institution(s)," is not included in our equation, because it is highly correlated with PH-18, "Number of placements outside the own home subsequent to the first is _____," which carries additional information that PH-24 does not.

The weights, such as the $-.24$ attached to PF-17 or the $-.01$ attached to PF-25 in the equation below, tell how much each variable is to be counted in our prediction of 0, 1, or 2 placement breakdowns or changes. It would be desirable to compare the weights directly to see how much a given predictor contributes to a prediction relative to another. Unfortunately, this procedure is generally not possible unless the scales and variances of the predictors are the same. Thus, since PF-17 and PF-63 are both on a response scale that runs from -2 to $+2$ and are essentially equally variable, we can say that the contribution of PF-17 is $-.24$ divided by $-.19$, or 1.26 that of PF-63. The same kind of direct com-

MANDY

Mandy is 17 years old, attractive and self-possessed. She has lived with her Casey foster family for four years.

Mandy's parents divorced when she was four. She hasn't seen her father since. Her mother periodically left her with relatives and would then return to make a home of sorts for her. By the time Mandy was eight, the home included a series of "uncles," and at the age of nine she was sexually abused by one of them. She began running away. She was taken from her mother and placed in a series of foster homes interspersed with group homes for delinquent children. When she was 13, she came to the attention of TCFP and became a Casey child.

Mandy's foster mother and father both work full-time and have one daughter. They had not intended to become foster parents, but the foster mother was asked by a friend in the state child welfare bureau to give temporary care to a young girl for whom no state facilities seemed to work. The parents agreed, but what was intended as a short-term arrangement became permanent. When TCFP accepted Mandy, the parents became Casey foster parents.

After Mandy entered the household at the age of 13, she ran away several times. It was her established way of getting out of any stressful or demanding situation, and her foster parents did and do require that she control her temper, obey household rules, and do her chores. She has not run away for three years now. She has developed an even disposition and good coping skills. She has a group of high-quality friends, and she has a boyfriend. She does somewhat above average work in school.

Mandy has developed good control of herself despite, or perhaps partly because of, the fact that her same-age foster-family sister does her best to keep Mandy off-balance, insecure, and unhappy. Having to share her parents for the first time at the age of 13 was very difficult, and she is not as socially adept as Mandy. The Casey support money and the fact that Mandy has a caseworker devoted to her welfare are also causes of jealousy. But Mandy seems to be able to handle the spite, and there is real cause to believe that, despite her stressful early years, Mandy will become a well-balanced, successful adult.

parison of either PF-17 or PF-63 to PF-25, however, cannot be made since the scale of the latter variable is a different one—years the foster parents have been married.

It is possible to put all the regression weights on a directly comparable scale by a procedure called "standardizing," but it has the disadvantage that the standardized weights may change greatly with respect to one another as even a single variable is added to or removed from the regression equation. Given this difficulty, we avoided trying to compare directly the relative contributions of the predictors to the outcome variable. The predictors are, however, listed in the regression equation in the order of their decreasing contribution of unique information to the prediction of number of placement breakdowns.

The following is the regression equation that resulted from stepdown analysis of the variables in table 13:

Number of placement breakdowns $= 0.53 - 0.24$ *PF-17* $- 0.19$ *PF-63*
$$- 0.01 \ PF\text{-}25 + 0.03 \ PH\text{-}18$$
$$+ 0.45 \ PH\text{-}29 + 0.76 \ PH\text{-}41$$

The regression equation is simply a formal mathematical statement that a prediction of the number of placement breakdowns or changes for a given child in the sample can be made as the sum of the regression constant (the number 0.53 in the equation above) plus the sum of the products of the weights times the values of the six respective predictor variables. Thus, the predicted number of placement breakdowns or changes for a given child would be the sum of the regression constant, 0.53, minus 0.24 times the rating of how strongly the foster father was emotionally involved with the child, minus 0.19 times the rating of how strongly the foster family manifested an overnurturing or smothering climate in its home, minus 0.01 times the number of years the foster parents had been married, plus 0.03 times the number of the child's foster placements outside the own home subsequent to the first before enrollment in TCFP, plus 0.45 times the judgment of whether or not passive-aggressive behavior was a child-related reason for placement breakdown(s) before enrollment in TCFP, plus 0.76 times the judgment of whether failure to attach was a risk factor in placements outside the own home subsequent to the first.

The values generated by this procedure should logically range from zero breakdowns to two breakdowns. Because the equation is based on a criterion that does not include this logical limitation in precise form, the numbers turned out to range in this case from slightly less than zero to slightly less than two. The whole number of predicted breakdown(s) is then simply whichever of 0, 1, or 2 the generated value is closest to. It should be noted that the regression constant mentioned above is an adjustment for the means of the predictor variables that keeps the predicted values within an appropriate range. The weights applied to the predictor variables are more commonly referred to as "regression coefficients" or, more exactly, as "partial regression coefficients."

The factors that pointed to placement stability in this regression equation were the foster father's emotional involvement with the child, the presence of an overnurturing or smothering environment in the foster home, and the foster parents having been married a longer rather than a shorter time. Factors pointing to placement breakdown were the foster child's having had many foster placements before entering TCFP, his or her having a tendency toward· passive-aggressive behavior, and having failed to attach in earlier foster placements.

Each of these factors can be turned around, of course, in terms of the prediction of placement maintenance or breakdown. That is, lack of emotional involvement on the part of the foster father, or the lack of an overnurturing climate in the foster home, or a shorter foster parent marriage all contribute to a prediction of placement breakdown. Similarly, a child's having had few or no foster placements before entering TCFP, his or her not having a tendency toward passive-aggressive behavior, and having attached in earlier foster placements all contribute to a prediction of placement maintenance. In discussing succeeding regression equations, we will not repeat this "turn around" aspect of the predictors, but it should be kept in mind in considering them.

From the point of view of a prescription for placement maintenance, three things are especially important, not only in and of themselves, but, given the nature of statistical procedure, because of the factors they are related to and implicitly carry along with them. The prescription includes a foster mother and father who are veterans of a number of years of marriage, the foster father's emotional involvement with the foster child, and an overnurturing, or even smothering, climate in the foster home. We may speculate again that, destructive as it might be for the own children of a family, an overnurturing or smothering climate signals the total support and acceptance a foster child may never have previously found.

Negative factors, ones that require special vigilance if placements are to be maintained, are passive-aggressive behavior, many previous foster placements, and failure to attach. No one working in foster care will be startled at our pinpointing these latter two indicators: children whose placements have failed before are likely to fail again, and inability to attach is a prime reason for placement failure. The importance of passive-aggressive behavior as a predictor of placement failure may provide a view, lacking previously, of the total undesirability of this response style.

Technical Considerations

The accuracy of the regression equation is generally measured as the proportion of the variability ("variance" in the formal statistical sense) of the outcome variable that can be accounted for by the predictors. Roughly, how close are the predictions to the actual values of the outcome variable? This proportion is symbolized as R^2 and was equal to .77 in this instance. Because multiple regression procedures tend to capitalize on chance variations within a given sample to produce the largest R^2 possible, it is customary to discount it by a factor that depends upon the sample size; that is, chance effects can be expected to be greater in smaller samples. The discounted or "shrunken" value of R^2 was 0.74. Even the shrunken value would ordinarily be considered quite large in behavioral or social science research. As will be illustrated below, all of the R^2 estimates in this study were large; this fact is discussed in more detail later.

A measure of prediction accuracy that may have more intuitive appeal is the number of "hits," or correct predictions of the actual number of placement breakdowns, made using the regression equation. By choosing our cutting points with care, we were able to classify correctly 45 out of 51, or 88 percent of the sample in terms of whether they had had 0, 1, or 2 placement breakdowns or changes while in TCFP. A hit rate of 88 percent is generally quite good by the standard of present-day social research, and the fact that it is biased in the upward direction by the selection of cutting points as well as by predictor variable selection provided us with an early impetus to replicate the findings with another sample of children to see how well the findings held up. It is not unknown for a high value of R^2 and a high hit rate based upon a relatively small sample of subjects to fall off to near-zero values upon cross-validation. Thus, we will avoid commenting on the predictive power of our regression equation until after the results of the cross validation are reported in the next chapter.

Outcome: Present Overall Level of Functioning of the Foster Child

The variables that correlated |.35| or more with the caseworker's rating of the present overall, global level of functioning of the foster child are listed in Table 14. Verbal statements of the relationships are given below. The strongest relationships between predictor variables and the child's overall level of functioning are stated first, followed by those that accounted for less variance.

Interpretation

PC-11. The more the child was rated as being unable to deal with success, the lower was his or her rated level of present overall functioning.

PC-8. The more the child was rated as being afraid of intimacy, the lower was his or her rated level of present overall functioning.

PC-15. The more the child was rated as having good social skills, the higher was his or her rated level of present overall functioning.

LOUIS

Louis is an intelligent, pleasant-looking young man of 14, unexceptional except for a somewhat closed manner. From the beginning he has had trouble holding on to a family. His mother deserted him shortly after birth, and he was formally adopted by a couple who had been unable to have children. By the time he was nine both his adoptive parents had become alcoholic. They divorced, and neither would provide a home for him. By the time of the ultimate dissolution of the adoptive family, the stresses and uncertainties of his life had made Louis suspicious, tentative in his relationships with others, and a habitual liar.

At this point Louis came to the attention of The Casey Family Program through state welfare officials. Because his adoptive grandmother had remained close to him, he was placed in a Casey foster family in her town. His habitual lying as well as his inability to form any emotional attachment to the family soon led to a placement breakdown. A second Casey placement was made, again in the same town to maintain the contact with his grandmother. This time he was not placed with a family, but rather with a woman who managed a group home for children who were in time-out from more traditional foster care. She was warm, but extremely firm and consistent in her behavior toward the children. She knew better than to expect trust or affection from Louis.

At present Louis has been in the group home for three years. He no longer habitually lies, but, if threatened, he prefers not to take a chance on the truth. He has had the same caseworker from his acceptance into the Program, and is a "high-maintenance" client: he sees his caseworker two or three times a week; otherwise he becomes edgy and uncomfortable. He does not, however, display much warmth toward the worker.

Louis has a talent for the piano and TCFP has underwritten twice-weekly lessons and his attendance at several music camps. He is kept as busy as possible around the home, particularly in its extensive garden during the summer. He is not demonstrative, but he does take most of his problems to the woman who runs the home, and seems to feel that she is on his side in his battles with life.

PC-19.   The more the child was rated as having athletic, musical, or similar skills, the higher was his or her rated level of present overall functioning.

PC-6.   The more the child was rated as being extremely needy of affection, the lower was his or her rated level of present overall functioning.

PF-62.   The better the foster family was rated in ability to tolerate unassimilated aspects of the foster child, such as symbolic retention of the

TABLE 14

Predictor Variables That Correlated |.35| or More with
the Caseworker's Rating of the Foster Child's
Present Overall Global Level of Functioning

	Variable	Correlation
PC-11	Child is unable to deal with success.	−.50
PC-8	Child is afraid of intimacy.	−.50
PC-15	Child has good social skills.	.43
PC-19	Child has athletic, musical, or similar skill.	.41
PC-6	Child is extremely needy of affection.	−.40
PF-62	The foster family can tolerate unassimilated aspects of the foster child, such as symbolic retention of the own parents.	.40
NF-39	Child has important relatives other than parents or siblings.	−.38
PF-58	A motivating and/or precipitating factor in taking a foster child into the home was liking children and/or a feeling of closeness to young people.	.37
NF-21	The biological father is known to have had a criminal record.	.37
PP-23	Child has ongoing contact with the father.	.36
PC-2	Child is passive-aggressive.	−.36
PF-72	Foster parents' overall attitude toward child is accepting and positive.	.35

biological parents, the higher was the child's rated level of present overall functioning.

NF-39. The more likely that a child had important relatives other than parents or siblings, the lower was his or her rated level of present overall functioning.

PF-58. The more that liking children and/or a feeling of closeness to young people was rated as a motivating and/or precipitating factor in taking a foster child into the home, the higher was the child's rated level of present overall functioning.

NF-21. The more likely that the biological father had a criminal record, the higher was the child's rated level of present overall functioning.

PP-23. The more likely that the child had ongoing contact with the biological father, the higher was the child's rated level of present overall functioning.

PC-2. The more the child was rated as passive-aggressive, the lower was the child's rated level of present overall functioning.

PF-72. The more the foster parents' overall attitude toward the child was rated as accepting and positive, the higher was the child's rated level of present overall functioning.

There were 12 predictors that correlated 1.351 or more with the caseworker's rating of the present overall, global level of functioning of the foster child. It is noteworthy that, while approximately the same proportion of predictors pertained to the child as did for placement maintenance, the predictors were of a quite different kind. For placement maintenance, the predictors concerned primarily the child's history: placement in an institution, failure to attach, and so on. But with respect to overall functioning, ratings of present personal characteristics came to the fore. Inability to deal with success, fear of intimacy, being needy of affection, and passive-aggressive behavior were negative indicators, and good social skills or an athletic, musical, or similar skill were positive ones.

There are several probable reasons why these ratings of personal characteristics correlated substantially with ratings of overall level of functioning. First, all were assessments of behavior made by caseworkers who had an intimate knowledge of the foster child and his or her situation. They saw and made connections between, for example, the employment of good social skills and episodes of good functioning, or between passive-aggressive behavior and instances of poor functioning.

There may also be something of a halo effect here, in that children exhibiting especially good social skills *this week*, for example, or showing themselves especially unable to deal with success *today*, are seen as *presently* functioning especially well or poorly, respectively, at an overall level. It is a bit of an oversimplification to speak of halo effects, however, because overall functioning is certainly composed of elements that include social skills, passive-aggressive behavior, and fear of intimacy.

Caseworkers' ratings of foster family characteristics were also closely related to their perceptions of the child's overall level of functioning. An accepting and positive attitude toward the foster child was an indicator that he or she was presently functioning at a good level. From a more causal point of view, a family that can tolerate unassimilated aspects of the child and that feels a special closeness to young people may be much more likely to foster a desirable level of overall functioning.

The relationships of the biological family to the child's overall level of functioning involve some paradoxes and a contradiction. First, the contradiction. Placement was more likely to be maintained if the biological father was not in contact with the child. But, as far as present overall level of functioning is concerned, higher functioning was associated with ongoing contact with the biological father. Briefly, the contradiction appears to be a false one. Let us make the reasonable assumption that contact with the biological father contributes to a child's overall level of functioning. But overall level of functioning and placement maintenance are not identical. A child whose functioning is supported at a high level through contact with the biological father may actively seek to end a placement that is less than satisfactory in an actualizing sense. And, of course, a child who is functioning effectively *and* who is in contact with his or her father may feel that if he or she demonstrates the inadequacy of the foster placement, the father will somehow reconstitute the own home or create a place for the child with him.

It appears paradoxical that a child with available important relatives other than parents or siblings would be rated as functioning at a poorer overall level. The support the relatives would offer might be supposed to increase a child's feelings of connectedness, of security and worth, and to help the child function at a higher overall level. After-the-fact discussions between the authors and Montana Division caseworkers led to the conclusion that there was some tendency for foster children with available relatives in addition to parents and siblings to push harder for return to a life with the parents and siblings and to make less effort at doing their best within the foster placement. The complexities in the situations of individual foster children, however, remind us that this explanation is not true across the board.

The relationship between better overall functioning and the biological father's having a criminal record is more straightforwardly explained. Five of the Montana Division foster children had a father with a criminal background. Three of these children were functioning at better than the average level, and the other two were at about the average level. Because none of them were below the average level, while many children whose fathers did not have a criminal record were, the correlation coefficient reached a level of .37. Although such a value is not large, it is one disadvantage of correlational methods that relatively modest effects can be reflected in values that seem appreciable. It was also true in this instance, however, that two of the three better-functioning foster children took a (perverse—but not to them) pride in their father's criminal exploits that may actually have contributed to feelings of self-worth and thus, indirectly, to a higher overall level of functioning. Therefore, this finding is more than artifactual, although, given the very small number of foster children involved, it would not be wise to generalize it beyond them.

The Regression Equation

Which of these variables provide the best prediction of the caseworker's rating of the present overall, global level of functioning of the foster child? The following regression equation resulted from stepdown analysis of the variables in Table 14:

Rating of overall functioning $= 4.17 - 0.15\ PC\text{-}2 - 0.46\ PC\text{-}6$
$$- 0.45\ PC\text{-}8 - 0.41\ PC\text{-}11$$
$$+ 0.26\ PC\text{-}15 + 0.36\ PC\text{-}19$$
$$+ 0.54\ PF\text{-}62 + 1.37\ PP\text{-}23$$
$$+ 1.06\ PF\text{-}72$$

Thus, the predicted rating of overall level of functioning for a given child in the sample would be the sum of the regression constant, 4.17, minus 0.15 times how passive-aggressive the child was rated, minus 0.46 times how needy of affection the child was rated, minus 0.45 times how afraid of intimacy the child was rated, minus 0.41 times how unable to deal with success the child was rated, plus 0.26 times how good the child's social skills were rated to be, plus 0.36 times the extent to which the child was rated as having athletic, musical, or similar skills, plus 0.54 times the rating of the foster family's ability to tolerate unassimilated aspects of the foster child, plus 1.37 times the value signifying that the child had ongoing contact with the biological father, plus 1.06 times how accepting and positive the foster parents were rated.

The values generated by this equation ranged from slightly less than 1.0 to slightly greater than 9.0. Values closer to 1 indicated poor functioning, while those closer to 9 indicated good functioning. A value close to 5 indicated middle-of-the-road levels of functioning that were neither particularly good nor particularly bad. The mean level of present overall functioning of the 51 children in our sample was rated 4.57, slightly less than the middle-of-the-road value, by the Montana Division caseworkers. Approximately two-thirds of the children were rated from 2 to 7, and the other third was about equally divided between 1's, those doing very poorly, and 8's and 9's, those doing very well.

The factors that pointed to a higher level of functioning in this regression equation were higher ratings of social skills and athletic, musical, or similar ability, the child's having contact with his or her biological father, and higher ratings of the foster family's ability to tolerate unassimilated aspects of the child, plus the extent to which they were rated as having an overall attitude toward the child that was accepting and positive.

The factors that pointed to a lower level of functioning were ratings that indicated the child was more passive-aggressive, more needy of affection, more afraid of intimacy, and less able to deal with success.

Our prescription for a high overall level of functioning would stress the foster child's having good social skills, athletic, musical, or similar skills, being in contact with the biological father, and being placed with a positive and accepting family that could tolerate unassimilated aspects of the child. Factors that would work against a child's achieving a higher overall level of functioning would center on the child with the loser outlook—unable to deal with success and afraid of intimacy—but needy of affection and afflicted with the passive-aggressive style. As before, given the nature of the statistical procedure, these positive and negative factors are important, not only in and of themselves, but also because of the factors they are related to and, through the stepdown regression procedures, implicitly carry along with them.

Technical Considerations

Recall that the accuracy of the regression equation is generally measured as the proportion of variance of the outcome variable that can be accounted for by the predicted values, or, roughly, the degree to which predicted values are comparable to the actual ratings of overall level of functioning. We symbolize this proportion as R^2. Here it was equal to 0.72. The shrunken value, the value discounted for chance occurrences that would tend to inflate its value in a sample of a particular size, was 0.65.

As with the R^2 for the prediction of placement breakdown or change, this is a very substantial value. Because such values commonly fall off to much more modest values upon replication, we will avoid commenting on the power of the regression equation until after we discuss the crossvalidation in the next chapter.

Outcome: Present Overall Level of Functioning of the Foster Family

The variables that correlated |.35| or more with the caseworker's rating of the present, overall global level of functioning of the foster family are listed in Table 15. Verbal statements of the relationships are given below. The strongest relationships between predictor variables and the foster family's overall level of functioning are stated first, followed by those that accounted for less variance.

Interpretation

PF-31. The more the foster parents were rated as exhibiting a high degree of comfort in their several roles, the higher was the rated level of present overall functioning of the foster family.

TABLE 15

*Predictor Variables That Correlated |.35| or More with
the Caseworker's Rating of the Present, Overall
Global Level of Functioning of
the Foster Family*

	Variable	Correlation
PF-31	The foster parents exhibit a high degree of comfort in their several roles.	.70
PF-58	A motivating and/or precipitating factor in taking a foster child into the home was liking children and/or a feeling of closeness to young people.	.68
PF-8	Foster mother possesses strong emotional coherence.	.66
PF-62	Foster family can tolerate unassimilated aspects of the foster child, such as symbolic retention of the own parents.	.62
PF-41	The foster family's ability to handle anger is good.	.56
PF-30	The foster parents have encouraged a physically affectionate family style.	.51
PF-39	The foster family's ability to share feelings is good.	.50
PF-40	The foster family's stress tolerance is high.	.48
PC-8	Child is afraid of intimacy.	−.45
PF-16	The foster father provides a strong male role model in the foster family.	.44
PF-9	The foster mother has earth mother as her dominant personal style.	.44
PF-37	The foster family's executive capacity is good.	.43
PF-34	The foster family works through problems to a conclusion.	.43
PP-26	Child has one sibling in the Program.	.40
PC-19	Child has athletic, musical, or similar skill.	.40
PF-43	The foster family's relationship to its own extended family is good.	.39
PF-65	The foster family is child-centered.	.38
PF-60	A motivating and/or precipitating factor in taking a foster child into the home was social commitment, as to a better world or to do something useful.	.38
PF-38	The foster family's ability to communicate under stress is good.	.37
PF-17	The foster father is emotionally involved with the child.	.36
PF-20	The foster child is intermediate in age with respect to the foster family's children.	.35

PF-58. The more that liking children and/or a feeling of closeness to young people was rated a motivating and/or precipitating factor in taking a foster child into the home, the higher was the rated level of present overall functioning of the foster family.

PF-8. The more the foster mother was rated as possessing strong emotional coherence, the higher was the rated level of present overall functioning of the foster family.

PF-62. The more the foster family was rated as able to tolerate unassimilated aspects of the foster child, such as symbolic retention of the biological parents, the higher was the rated level of overall functioning of the foster family.

PF-41. The more the foster family's ability to handle anger was rated as good, the higher was the rated level of present overall functioning of the foster family.

PF-30. The more the foster parents were rated as having encouraged a physically affectionate family style, the higher was the rated level of present overall functioning of the foster family.

PF-39. The more the ability of the foster family to share feelings was rated as good, the higher was the rated level of present overall functioning of the foster family.

PF-40. The more the stress tolerance of the foster family was rated as high, the higher was the rated level of present overall functioning of the foster family.

PC-8. The more the child was rated as fearing intimacy, the lower was the rated level of present overall functioning of the foster family.

PF-16. The more the foster father was rated as providing a strong male role model, the higher was the rated level of present overall functioning of the foster family.

PF-9. The more the foster mother was rated as having the earth mother as her dominant style, the higher was the rated level of present overall functioning of the foster family.

PF-37. The more the executive capacity of the foster family was rated as good, the higher was the rated level of present overall functioning of the foster family.

PF-34. The more the foster family was rated as working through problems to a conclusion, the higher was the rated level of present overall functioning of the foster family.

PP-26. The more likely it was that the child had one sibling in the Program, the higher was the rated level of present overall functioning of the foster family.

PC-19. The more the child was rated as having an athletic, musical, or similar skill, the higher was the rated level of present overall functioning of the foster family.

PF-43.   The more the foster family's relationship to its own extended family was rated as good, the higher was the rated level of present overall functioning of the foster family.

PF-65.   The more the foster family was rated as child-centered, the higher was the rated level of present overall functioning of the foster family.

PF-60.   The more that social commitment, as to a better world or to do something useful, was rated as a motivating and/or precipitating factor in taking a foster child into the home, the higher was the rated level of present overall functioning of the foster family.

PF-38.   The more the ability of the foster family to communicate under stress was rated as good, the higher was the rated level of present overall functioning of the foster family.

PF-17.   The more the foster father was rated as emotionally involved with the child, the higher was the rated level of present overall functioning of the foster family.

PF-20.   The greater the likelihood that the foster child was intermediate in age with respect to the foster family's children, the higher was the rated level of present overall functioning of the foster family.

As the nature of the outcome variable would lead us to expect, 18 of the 21 predictors that correlated |.35| or more with the overall level of the foster family focused on characteristics of the foster mother, the foster father, or the foster family. The four predictors that had most in common with the overall functioning of the foster family related to the comfort of the foster parents in their several roles, to their being motivated to take a foster child by a genuine liking for children, to the foster mother possessing strong emotional coherence, and to the ability of the foster family to tolerate unassimilated aspects of the child. Thus, emotional strength, comfort with themselves, openness, and tolerance would seem to be the characteristics most clearly associated with high-functioning foster parents.

In addition to strong emotional coherence, the earth mother style with its encompassing love and acceptance was another clear characteristic of the foster family that was functioning well on an overall, global level. The foster father in such a family provided a strong masculine role model, presumably backed by enough self-confidence to allow him not only to be emotionally involved with the child but to show it as well.

Also associated with a high-functioning foster family was having the foster child be intermediate in age with respect to the foster family's children. Many foster care professionals have argued that bracketing a foster child with foster family children both younger and older helps provide him or her with role definition and acceptable limits on behavior, and our results would support such a contention.

In addition to being comfortable in their several roles, foster parents who encouraged a physically affectionate family style were generally rated as functioning at a higher overall level. These families tended to have good relationships with their own extended family. They handled anger well and had a high stress tolerance. They were also good and determined communicators and problem solvers. They were motivated to take a foster child into their home not only because they liked children and felt close to them, but also out of a sense of social commitment that may have been a basic component of their ability to tolerate unassimilated aspects of the foster child. Their homes were seen as child-centered.

It may be instructive to note some of the factors that did *not* characterize high-functioning foster parents. Neither age nor education nor birth order made a difference; nor did employment, attaining financial security, length of marriage, or who initiated taking the foster child into the home. Spiritual orientation and experience with death and grief were not important. Changes in family structure or household had little association with level of functioning, nor did association with others who were involved with foster care, or social class, or rural or urban setting, or geographic location within the state. Thus, it is a fair summary to say that demographic and social structural variables were much less closely associated with a high level of overall foster family functioning than were variables that reflected the personality and style of the foster parents.

Three characteristics of the foster child were associated with higher levels of functioning in foster families. Having a sibling in TCFP was one such characteristic. It is tempting to speculate that a child with a sibling in the Program felt more secure in his or her placement and had higher expectations for its success.

A child with an athletic, musical, or similar skill was associated with higher-functioning foster families. The data did not allow us to determine clearly whether in general the child brought the developed skill with him or her to the foster family or whether it was nurtured within the family environment.

The child's fear of intimacy was associated with lower levels of overall foster family functioning. It is tempting to hypothesize that a child who would not allow himself or herself to become emotionally close to the foster family was capable of disrupting its emotional integrity and lowering its level of functioning.

The Regression Equation

Which of these variables provide the best prediction of the case-worker's rating of the present, overall global level of functioning of the foster family? They are given, according to the stepdown procedure, in the regression equation based on the variables in Table 15 as:

Rating of family functioning $= 5.41 - 0.34\ PC\text{-}8 + 0.41\ PF\text{-}16$
$$+ 0.92\ PF\text{-}31 + 0.38\ PF\text{-}65$$
$$+ 0.66\ PF\text{-}62 + 0.68\ PF\text{-}58$$
$$- 0.43\ PF\text{-}40$$

Thus, the predicted rating of overall level of functioning of a specific family in our sample would be the sum of the regression constant, 5.41, minus 0.34 times the rating of the child's fear of intimacy, plus 0.41 times how strong a masculine role model the foster father was rated as providing, plus 0.92 times how high a degree of comfort in their several roles the foster parents were rated as exhibiting, plus 0.38 times the degree to which the foster home was rated as child-centered, plus 0.66 times how well the foster family was rated as being able to tolerate unassimilated aspects of the foster child, plus 0.68 times the degree to which a liking for young people was rated a motivating and/or precipitating factor in taking a foster child into the home, minus 0.43 times the degree to which the stress tolerance of the foster family was rated as high.

The values generated by this equation ranged from slightly greater than 1.0 to slightly greater than 9.0. Values closer to 1.0 indicated poor functioning, while those closer to 9.0 indicated good functioning. A value close to 5.0 indicated a middle-of-the-road level of functioning that was neither particularly good nor particularly bad. The present overall level of functioning for the 51 families in the sample was rated 5.92, somewhat above the middle-of-the-road value, by the Montana Division case-workers. About two-thirds of the families were rated from 4 to 8, and the other third was about equally divided between 1's, 2's and 3's, those doing quite poorly, and 9's, those doing quite well.

The predictors that pointed to a higher level of functioning in this regression equation were generally oriented toward the foster family's style. They included the degree of comfort of the foster parents in their several roles, the degree to which the foster home was child-centered, the presentation of a strong masculine role model by the foster father, the ability of the foster family to tolerate unassimilated aspects of the foster child, and liking for children having been a motivating and/or precipitating factor in taking a foster child into the family. Emotional strength, comfort within themselves, tolerance, and liking for young people would seem to be the characteristics most useful in predicting a high level of functioning by the foster parents.

One predictor that pointed to a lower level of functioning was a rating that indicated the child was afraid of intimacy. The other was a high rating of the family's ability to tolerate stress. A negative weight on this variable appears contradictory, especially when, as pointed out above, it correlates positively with higher levels of overall family functioning. What we are seeing is an instance of the regression procedure including unique information, the basis for which is not obvious. *Given the other six variables in the equation,* higher stress tolerance by the foster family is related to lower levels of overall functioning. Why this is so is not apparent—it is the outcome of a complex set of relationships among the predictors that we will not, given the relatively small size of the sample, attempt to explicate. The usual tools for such explication include partial and semipartial correlation, which are more trustworthy with larger samples. It should be emphasized that we are not arguing that a counterintuitive relationship exists here, but only that, *given the other six variables included in the equation and the set of linear relationships among all seven predictors,* high stress tolerance was associated with lower levels of overall foster family functioning.

Technical Considerations

The value of R^2 for our prediction of present level of overall global functioning of the foster family was 0.86. The shrunken value was 0.84. We will comment on the predictive power of the regression equation after discussing the cross-validation in the next chapter.

Outcome: Caseworker's Willingness to Choose the Family Again

The variables that correlated |.35| or more with the caseworker's rating of his or her willingness to place a child, although not necessarily the same one, with the same foster family if the choice were to be made again on the basis of present knowledge are listed in Table 16. Verbal statements of the relationships are given below. The strongest relationships between predictor variables and willingness to choose the family again are stated first, followed by those that accounted for less variance.

TABLE 16

Predictor Variables That Correlated |.35| or More with Caseworker's Willingness to Choose the Foster Family Again

	Variable	Correlation
PF-8	Foster mother possesses strong emotional coherence.	.64
PF-38	The foster family's ability to communicate under stress is good.	.63
PF-32	The foster parents' personal interaction is one of ease.	.62
PF-3	Educational level of foster mother.	.61
PF-41	The foster family's ability to handle anger is good.	.59
PF-39	The foster family's ability to share feelings is good.	.58
PF-65	The foster family is child-centered.	.55
PF-68	The foster family lives in a geographic location (in the state) similar to that of the biological family.	.52
PF-62	The foster family can tolerate unassimilated aspects of the foster child, such as symbolic retention of the biological parents.	.49
PF-13	Educational level of foster father.	.49
NF-39	Child has important relatives other than parents or siblings.	.45
PF-51	A motivating and/or precipitating factor in taking a foster child into the home was being "Casey long-term."	.41
NF-43	Child has no present contacts with relatives other than siblings.	−.41
PF-34	The foster family works through problems to a conclusion.	.40
PF-44	The foster family maintains generational boundaries within itself and its extended family.	.39
PH-5	Child's first placement outside their own home was with relatives or family friends.	.37
NF-21	Biological father is known to have had a criminal record.	−.36
PF-37	The foster family's executive capacity is good.	.35
PF-64	There is competition between foster parents for the affection of the child.	−.35

Interpretation

PF-8. The more the foster mother was rated as possessing strong emotional coherence, the greater was the willingness of the caseworker to place a child with the same foster family if the choice were to be made again on the basis of present knowledge.

PF-38. The more the ability of the foster family to communicate under stress was rated as good, the greater was the willingness of the caseworker to place a child with the same foster family if the choice were to be made again on the basis of present knowledge.

PF-32. The more the personal interaction of the foster parents was rated as one of ease, the greater was the willingness of the caseworker to place a child with the same foster family if the choice were to be made again on the basis of present knowledge.

PF-3. The higher the educational level of the foster mother, the greater was the willingness of the caseworker to place a child with the same foster family if the choice were to be made again on the basis of present knowledge.

PF-41. The more the ability of the foster family to handle anger was rated as good, the greater was the willingness of the caseworker to place a child with the same foster family if the choice were to be made again on the basis of present knowledge.

PF-39. The more the ability of the foster family to share feelings was rated as good, the greater was the willingness of the caseworker to place a child with the same foster family if the choice were to be made again on the basis of present knowledge.

PF-65. The more the foster family was rated as child-centered, the greater was the willingness of the caseworker to place a child with the same foster family if the choice were to be made again on the basis of present knowledge.

PF-68. The more likely it was that the foster family lived in a geographic location (in the state) similar to the own family, the greater was the willingness of the caseworker to place a child with the same foster family if the choice were to be made again on the basis of present knowledge.

PF-62. The more the foster family was rated as able to tolerate unassimilated aspects of the foster child such as symbolic retention of the own parents, the greater was the willingness of the caseworker to place a child with the same foster family if the choice were to be made again on the basis of present knowledge.

PF-13. The higher the educational level of the foster father, the greater was the willingness of the caseworker to place a child with the same foster family if the choice were to be made again on the basis of present knowledge.

NF-39. The more likely it was that the child had important relatives other than parents or siblings, the greater was the willingness of the caseworker to place a child with the same foster family if the choice were to be made again on the basis of present knowledge.

PF-51. The more that taking a foster child into the home was rated as being based on the family's being "Casey long-term," the greater was the willingness of the caseworker to place a child with the same foster family if the choice were to be made again on the basis of present knowledge.

NF-43. The more likely it was that the child had no present contacts with relatives other than siblings, the less was the willingness of the caseworker to place a child with the same foster family if the choice were to be made again on the basis of present knowledge.

PF-34. The more the foster family was rated as working problems through to a conclusion, the greater was the willingness of the caseworker to place a child with the same foster family if the choice were to be made again on the basis of present knowledge.

PF-44. The more the foster family was rated as maintaining generational boundaries within itself and its extended family, the greater was the willingness of the caseworker to place a child with the same foster family if the choice were to be made again on the basis of present knowledge.

PH-5. The more likely it was that the child's first placement outside the own home was with relatives or family friends, the greater was the willingness of the caseworker to place a child with the same foster family if the choice were to be made again on the basis of present knowledge.

NF-21. The greater the likelihood that the biological father was known to have had a criminal record, the less willing was the caseworker to place a child with the same foster family if the choice were to be made again on the basis of present knowledge.

PF-37. The more the executive capacity of the foster family was rated as good, the greater was the willingness of the caseworker to place a child with the same foster family if the choice were to be made again on the basis of present knowledge.

PF-64. The more the foster parents were rated as competing for the child's affection, the less willing was the caseworker to place a child with the same foster family if the choice were to be made again on the basis of present knowledge.

Once again, the emotional coherence of the foster mother and an easy personal interaction between the foster parents were among the predictors most highly related to the outcome variable. The ability of the foster parents to get along with each other, probably grounded in the solid emotional base of the foster mother, was a characteristic that told the caseworker that they could also get along with a foster child.

At essentially the same level of importance were the ability to communicate under stress, to handle anger, and to share feelings. The recognition seems implicit in these relationships that accepting a Casey Family Program child will be stressful to the foster family and that the ability to get a handle on that stress, and any accompanying anger, and to be able to communicate in such a situation are of great importance.

A child-centered home and the capacity of the foster family to tolerate unassimilated aspects of the foster child were also closely related to the caseworker's willingness to choose a foster family again. It seems evident that the ability to accept a child as he or she is signifies to Montana Division caseworkers a foster home that is likely to be successful in nurturing a foster child.

Although the educational level of the foster mother and foster father and their geographical location in the state have not been associated with other outcome measures, they correlated substantially with the willingness of the caseworker to choose a foster family again. It is probably the greater ease of communication with better-educated foster parents that makes this an attractive characteristic to caseworkers. In the same way, having the foster parents situated in the same geographic areas as the biological parents may facilitate transactions that involve both parties.

Our discussions with Montana Division caseworkers clarified their general feeling that foster children with relatives of importance to them in addition to parents and siblings had better long-term prospects. Hence their willingness to choose foster families again for children who had such biological family resources to begin with: those placements had worked out better than the average. Similarly a child whose first placement outside the own home was with relatives or family friends had a better chance of being gently treated and better long-term prospects. Although a few children whose fathers had criminal records had done better than average in overall functioning, the complex picture and prospects these children presented probably kept most placements from being the type that the caseworker wanted to repeat.

Foster family managerial characteristics that were related to caseworkers' desire to choose them again were good executive capacity and the ability to work problems through to a conclusion. These foster parents were also more likely to maintain generational boundaries in their extended family.

"Casey long-term" is essentially another name for foster parents whom caseworkers would be especially likely to choose again, particularly for a difficult child.

Foster parents who competed for the child's affection had a low likelihood of being chosen again.

The Regression Equation

Which subset of these variables provided the best prediction of the caseworker's willingness to place a child with the same foster family if the choice were to be made again on the basis of present knowledge? The following regression equation resulted from stepdown analysis of the variables in Table 16:

Willingness to choose again = $-0.88 + 0.44$ *PF-8* $+ 0.25$ *PF-38*
$$+ 0.32 \text{ } PF\text{-}68 + 0.41 \text{ } PF\text{-}65$$
$$+ 0.55 \text{ } NF\text{-}39 - 0.47 \text{ } NF\text{-}21$$
$$- 0.19 \text{ } PF\text{-}64$$

Thus, the rated willingness of the caseworker to choose a particular family again would be the sum of the regression constant, -0.88, plus 0.44 times how strong the foster mother's emotional coherence was rated, plus 0.25 times how good the ability of the foster family to communicate under stress was rated, plus 0.32 times the likelihood that the foster family lived in a geographical location (in the state) similar to the biological family, plus 0.41 times how child-centered the foster family was rated, plus 0.55 times the likelihood that the child had important relatives other than parents or siblings, minus 0.47 times the likelihood that the biological father had had a criminal record, minus 0.19 times the degree to which the foster parents were rated as being in competition for the affection of the child.

The values generated by this equation ranged from slightly less than -2 to slightly more than 2. Values closer to -2 indicated that the caseworker would be quite reluctant to choose the foster family again; those closer to 2 indicated that the worker would be quite likely to choose the family again. A value close to 0 indicated that the caseworker had no particular feelings, either positive or negative, about choosing the foster family again. On the -2 to 2 scale, the mean caseworker rating of willingness to choose the foster family again was 0.28, slightly more than the middle value on the scale. Approximately 50 percent of the foster families were rated -1, 0 or $+1$, with about 10 percent more being rated $+$ than -1. The other half were approximately equally divided between -2's, those who would definitely not be chosen again, and 2's, those who would definitely be chosen again.

The factors that were associated with a caseworker's willingness to choose a foster family again were the foster mother's emotional coherence, the foster family's being child-centered, able to communicate under stress, living in a geographical area (in the state) similar to the biological parents, and the child's having important relatives other than parents or siblings. These variables seem to be a pragmatic mix of a good foster family, a convenient location, and the possibility of a biological family support system.

The factors that were contraindicative for the caseworker were the biological father's having had a criminal record and competition between the foster parents for the child's affection. These two variables, along with the ones implicitly carried along by the stepdown procedure, may represent a prescription for a child who carries little negative baggage associated with his or her own family into the foster placement, and a foster family that does not set up notable conflicts in the child.

Technical Considerations

The value of R^2 for this regression equation was 0.86. The shrunken value was 0.84. We will discuss the predictive power of the equation after considering the cross-validation of these findings in the following chapter.

Relationships Among Outcome Variables

The correlations among the primary outcome variables and of the primaries with the secondary outcome variable are given in Table 17. They range from a value of .55, denoting a substantial degree of overlap, to $-.02$, indicating almost complete independence. Three pairs of variables are related in important ways.

Placement breakdown or change is moderately negatively correlated $(-.39)$ with the overall level of functioning of the foster family. The better the rated functioning of the foster family, the fewer placement breakdowns occurred. Placement breakdown showed only small negative correlations, $-.22$ and $-.23$, respectively, with the child's overall level of functioning and the willingness of the caseworker to choose the foster family again.

The overall level of functioning of the child and the overall functioning of the foster family were substantially positively correlated (.55). The higher the rated overall level of functioning of the child, the higher was the rated overall level of functioning of the foster family. The child's level of functioning exhibited almost no relationship $(-.02)$ to the willingness of the caseworker to choose the family again.

Finally, the overall level of functioning of the foster family was moderately positively correlated (.44) with the willingness of the caseworker to choose the family again. The higher the rated level of overall functioning of the foster family, the greater was the willingness of the caseworker to choose the family again.

Overall, placement breakdown or change was least related to the other outcome measures. Since the others all involved ratings, this result is not surprising. Placement breakdown was not unrelated to the other outcome measures, however. It is moderately negatively correlated with the level of functioning of the foster family. As would be expected, there

TABLE 17

Correlations Among Outcome Variables

		Primary			Secondary
		PBD	COF	FOF	CFA
PBD	Placement Breakdown	—	− .22	− .39	− .23
COF	Child's Overall Functioning		—	.55	− .02
FOF	Family's Overall Functioning			—	.44
	CFA, Choose Family Again				—

were fewer breakdowns or changes in foster families with higher rated levels of functioning.

The overall level of functioning of the child was strongly linked to the level of functioning of the family. Given the lower level of the correlation of the child's overall functioning with placement breakdown, we find objective support for the intuitive conclusion that the foster family occupies the central position in the foster care paradigm. Without it, foster care does not exist, and the better it functions, the more positive the other outcomes.

This reasoning is further supported by the fact that the outcome measure most closely related to the caseworker's willingness to choose the foster family again was the overall level of functioning of the foster family. It appears that Jim Casey's insistence upon the importance of finding strong foster families was well founded.

Although the level of functioning of the foster family seems to be the most central outcome measure, and although there are at least three linkages among pairs of outcome variables that are worthy of note, it appears that all four are sufficiently independent of the others to justify the attention we have focused on them individually and to make it worthwhile to carry our examination a step further.

Before we proceed with that, however, let us use the information from our outcome measures to make some brief quantitative judgments about the care provided by the Montana Division of The Casey Family Program. To begin with, it appears that the ratings of overall functioning of foster children and foster families were hardheaded ones and not achieved with the help of rose-colored glasses. On a nine-point scale where 1 signified extremely poor functioning, 5 meant middle-of-the-road functioning that was neither very poor nor very good, and 9 referred to extremely good functioning, the average ratings assigned Montana Division foster children and foster families, respectively, were 4.57 and 5.92, with no substantial skewing of the distributions. On the average, the children were rated as functioning at a somewhat less than average level, as one would expect, given their histories. On the average, the foster families were functioning at a better than average level, as one would expect, given the care that went into their selection. Even given the somewhat better than average functioning they displayed, however, the caseworkers' willingness to choose the families again, not necessarily for the same child and with full benefit of hindsight, was only slightly above the indifference point. They were favorable on the whole toward their foster families, but they worked with the continuing attitude that better foster families could be found and that better choices for particular children could be made.

The choices, in terms of placement breakdown or change, had been good. Of 51 children in the present sample, 14 had suffered a breakdown or change while in TCFP, and of these, only seven had had more than one such breakdown or change. A 73 percent rate of placement maintenance is, by the standards of almost any public agency, excellent. To do them justice, however, no public agency the authors are aware of has the resources or the freedom of action and initiative enjoyed by TCFP. It is also true that the children of the Montana Division had been under TCFP care for periods varying from a few months to many years, and, as would be expected, the likelihood of a placement breakdown or change showed a modest tendency ($r = .30$) to increase with the number of years that a child had been enrolled in the program.

Overall, the professional staff of the Montana Division had selected those underachievers in foster care in whom Jim Casey was so interested, it had placed them with foster families who were functioning well, and, in nearly three out of every four instances, those placements had been maintained for a substantial period of time. To the extent that stable placements contribute to the development of foster children who will be emancipated into a more successful adult life, the efforts of the Montana Division have been markedly successful.

Predictors Common to More than One Outcome Variable

We will now try to extend our understanding of the specific variables associated with positive and negative outcomes of foster care within TCFP by examining those variables that were related to more than one outcome measure. We asked whether there were predictors that were consistently related to positive and negative placement outcomes. What factors were important enough to predict outcome measures that enjoyed a moderate to substantial degree of independence from one another?

A total of 50 predictors were related to the outcome measures at the |.35| or greater level. The 15 that correlated greater than or equal to |.35| with more than one outcome variable are shown in Table 18, which also indicates the predictors that entered one or more regression equations.

Interpretation

In terms of correlating |.35| or more with all four outcome measures and entering two regression equations, the most powerful predictor was the ability of the foster family to tolerate unassimilated aspects of the foster child. Thus, the capacity to get along with, if not to accept, the aspects of the child that are oriented outside the foster family and are without regard to its organization and well-being may be the best single indicator of a potentially successful foster placement.

The foster home's being child-centered was correlated |.35| or more with three outcome variables and entered two regression equations. An overall orientation toward an involvement with children seems to be a sine qua non of a good foster family. Only slightly less important was the emotional coherence of the foster mother. This predictor was related to three outcome measures and entered one regression equation.

All three of the above-mentioned predictors correlated substantially, that is, |.35| or more, with both placement breakdown or change and the level of functioning of the foster family, the most central outcome variable. Thus, it is reasonable to think of them as the three factors most closely related to placement success in the Montana Division of TCFP: ability to tolerate unassimilated aspects of the foster child, a child-centered foster home, and a foster mother with the emotional coherence necessary to keep the home functioning on an even keel.

The foster child's fear of intimacy was a strong negative indicator of placement success. It correlated |.35| or more with two outcome measures and entered both regression equations. A foster child who is fearful of establishing close personal relationships within the context of a foster family is a very poor bet for placement success.

Six predictors correlated |.35| or more with two outcome measures and entered one regression equation. As the common wisdom in foster care has it, a child with athletic, musical, or similar skills is a better bet than one without such skills, other things being more or less equal. The emotional involvement of the foster father with the child was important. Unless the foster father had made a commitment to the child that had a

TABLE 18

Predictor Variables That Correlated |.35| or More with More than One Outcome Variable*

	Item	Outcome Variable			
		PBD	FOC	FOF	CFA
PF-62	Family can tolerate unassimilated aspects of foster child.	+	+*	+*	+
PF-65	Foster home is child-centered.	+		+*	+*
PF-8	Foster mother possesses strong emotional coherence.	+		+	+*
PC-8	Child is afraid of intimacy.		+*	+*	
PC-19	Child has athletic, musical, or similar skill.		+*	+	
PF-17	Foster father is emotionally involved with the child.	+*		+	
PF-38	Foster family's ability to communicate under stress is good.			+	+*
PF-58	Motivating and/or precipitating factor was liking children or feeling closeness to young people.		+	+*	
NF-21	Biological father was known to have had a criminal record.		+		+*
NF-39	Child has important relatives other than parents or siblings.		+		+*
PF-34	Foster family works through problems to a conclusion.			+	+
PF-37	Foster family's executive capacity is good.			+	+
PF-39	Foster family's ability to share feelings is good.			+	+
PF-41	Foster family's ability to handle anger is good.			+	+
PF-43	Foster family's relationship to its own extended family is good.		+		+

*Indicates that the predictor entered the regression equation for the outcome variable.

genuine emotional component, good outcomes were not as likely. Liking for children and a feeling of closeness to them was perhaps the most important motivating and/or precipitating factor in taking a foster child into the home; that is, the best reason for taking on foster children is because you like children. Other factors such as social commitment are important, but this one may be the best indicator of placement success. A foster child who had relatives of importance to him or her besides parents and siblings was more likely to enjoy a successful placement. "The more the merrier" may not be a correct statement of this relationship; "the more

SAM

Sam is a sturdy, extremely strong child of nine. He is a good-looking boy and on short acquaintance can be charming, but his perceptions of the world are skewed. He has very little control over a fierce temper, and that, along with his abnormal strength, makes him very difficult to handle.

Sam's mother and father divorced when he was three. His mother was periodically delusional, and intermixed fundamentalist Christianity with demonic visions. She preached a strong mixture of both to Sam, and, before she died of cancer when he was six, told him that she would be going to heaven and watching him. Three years later, Sam will still ask acquaintances if his mother is in heaven, and if there are demons.

When Sam's mother died, his father tried to make a home for him, but the boy proved too much for him to handle. Sam was placed in several foster homes by the state, but he was so out of control and his ideas so strange that each placement broke down in a very short time.

When he was seven, Sam came under TCFP care. He was given a thorough psychological workup, and the results indicated that it might still be possible to turn him in a more normal direction. He was placed in a foster home with a permanently working mother, a seasonally employed father, and a son three years older than he. Sam was with them for two years. His caseworker spent a lot of time with Sam and the family. As anyone involved with him could attest, being around Sam was extremely stressful; in addition, the family generated considerable stress for itself. The caseworker tried to help the family become better problem solvers, both for their sake and so that Sam would have a stable home. But though Sam more or less held his own in his contact with reality, he was not improving, and as he grew older and stronger, it became harder to handle him.

At the end of two years, the foster family itself began to fall apart. They used Sam as a scapegoat, and the father's physical punishment of him became excessive. The older child taunted Sam and treated him with contempt, and the mother began to talk of leaving the family.

Sam was removed from the foster home and placed in a closed institution. But he is still a "Casey child," and TCFP continues to provide financial support and professional care to give what potential he has a chance to develop.

the stabler" may be closer. Finally, a biological father who had a criminal record seemed to be a potent influence on placement success. Depending on the context, it may be either positive or negative, but it is a predictor that one cannot afford to ignore in that relatively small fraction of foster children to whom it applies.

Five foster family variables correlated |.35| or more with two outcome measures, although none of them entered a regression equation. Two of them were associated with decision making and problem solving: good executive capacity and the ability to work problems through to a conclusion. Two had to do with emotional communication: the ability to share feelings and to handle anger. The last points to a family that understands families; that is, one whose relationship to its own extended family is good.

Although it is not listed in the table, passive-aggressive behavior in two different contexts, as a general descriptor of the child and as a risk factor in placements subsequent to the first outside the own home, correlated |.35| or more with two outcome variables. In both cases it entered the regression equation.

In discussing the predictors in this context, we are ignoring the magnitude of their correlations with particular outcome variables and concentrating on how many outcome measures they are tied to. Thus, we have spoken of "placement success" and "successful outcomes" rather than of more specific measures. In that sense, our generalizations go beyond the data in this discussion, but we feel that the outcome measures provide a reasonable mapping of the larger variable, "placement success," and that our conclusions are supported by our data.

Two Additional Outcome-Related Variables

Before considering additional technical problems with our statistical methods and the matter of cross-validation, there are two other outcome-related measures on which data were collected for their potential in program planning. Because we were interested in factors that might be associated with entry into TCFP at an earlier or later age, we found the correlation between the predictors and age at entry. Given the preference of TCFP for children with more difficult and deprived backgrounds, we were in a sense asking what the most common threads in that fabric of hard times might be. In a somewhat narrower focus than age at entry provides, we sought the factors that were most closely correlated with the number of placements the child had before entering TCFP. This variable has some slightly shaky underpinnings in that not every placement change was associated with a breakdown or failure. Some were made for administrative purposes or even convenience, and the records available to us were not always clear in this regard. In coding this variable, we added every placement a child had before admission to TCFP unless it was absolutely clear that a given placement change was *not* due to breakdown.

Age at Entry to TCFP

The variables that correlated |.35| or more with age at entry into TCFP are listed in Table 19. As with the primary and secondary outcome measures, verbal statements of the relationships are given below, and the strongest relationships are given first.

Interpretation

DC-2.   The older the child, the older he or she was at entry to TCFP.

RF-11.   The more likely it was that the child had been put at risk by a caregiver, the younger he or she was at entry to TCFP.

PP-27.   The more likely it was that the child had more than one sibling in the Program, the younger he or she was at entry to TCFP.

NF-2.   The more likely it was that the parents were divorced, the older was the child at entry to TCFP.

PH-1.   The older the child was at the time of the first placement outside the home, the older he or she was at entry to TCFP.

NF-24.   The more likely it was that the father failed to accept the child, and/or had no relationship with the child, and/or rejected the child, the younger the child was at entry to TCFP.

PH-45.   The more likely it was that a risk factor in placements outside the home subsequent to the first placement was foster family disruption, the younger was the child at entry to TCFP.

DC-1.   The more likely it was that the child's race was other or unknown, the younger he or she was at entry to TCFP.

DC-5.   The more likely that the child's religious affiliation was Catholic, the younger he or she was at entry to TCFP.

Two of the variables that correlated with age at entry were related to it in ways that are somewhat definitional. With respect to DC-2, older children were more likely to have entered the Program at a later age, given that the Program has a limited history in Montana. In a similar way, the older the child was at first placement outside the own home, the older he or she would (usually) be at subsequent entry to TCFP.

Neglect, rejection by the biological father, and family disruption in an early foster placement were factors that contributed to putting the child in such straits that earlier rather than later entry to the Program was called for.

A child with more than one sibling in TCFP was more likely to enter at a younger age. This finding is primarily a matter of the Program's becoming aware of an eligible child at an early age through providing care for older siblings.

TABLE 19

Variables That Correlated |.35| or More with Age at Entry to TCFP

	Variable	Correlation
DC-2	Child is ——— years of age.	.84
RF-11	Child was put at risk by neglect by caregiver.	−.45
PP-27	Child has more than one sibling in the Program.	−.44
NF-2	Parents are divorced.	.39
PH-1	Child's age at first placement was ——— years.	.39
NF-24	Father is known to have failed to accept the child, and/or to have had no relationship with the child, and/or to have rejected the child.	−.39
PH-45	Risk factor in placements outside the home subsequent to the first was foster family disruption.	−.36
DC-1	Child's race is other or unknown.	−.36
DC-5	Child has religious affiliation of Catholic.	−.35

Children of unusual (in Montana) or unknown racial background tended to be accepted into the Program at an earlier age. It seems likely that these children had fewer opportunities for adoption or foster placement sponsored by public agencies and became prime candidates for TCFP.

Children of Catholic religious affiliation and those whose natural parents were not divorced tended to be accepted at an earlier age.

Number of Placements Before Entering TCFP

The variables that correlated |.35| or more with number of placements before entering TCFP are listed in Table 20. Verbal statements of the relationships are given below. The strongest relationships are given first.

Interpretation

NF-20.   The more likely it was that the father had an alcohol abuse problem, the greater was the number of placements before entering TCFP.

RF-14.   The more likely it was that the child was put at risk by alcohol problems in the family generally, the greater was the number of placements before entering TCFP.

TABLE 20

Variables That Correlated |.35| or More With Number of Placements Before Entering TCFP

Variable		Correlation
NF-20	Biological father is known to have had an alcohol abuse problem.	.61
RF-14	Child was put at risk by alcohol problems in the family.	.56
PH-30	Child-related reason for placement breakdown(s) before entering TCFP was running away.	.43
NF-22	Father is known to have been hospitalized or to be deceased.	.42
PH-47	Risk factor in placements outside the own home subsequent to the first was the nature of the placements themselves.	.39
RT-8	Child's response to threat is running away.	.38
PH-24	Child had one or more placement(s) in institution(s).	.38

PH-30. The more likely it was that a child-related reason for placement breakdown(s) before entering TCFP was running away, the greater was the number of placements before admission to TCFP.

NF-22. The more likely it was that the father had been hospitalized or deceased, the greater was the number of placements before entering TCFP.

PH-47. The more likely it was that the nature of the placements themselves was a risk factor in placements outside the natural home subsequent to the first, the greater was the number of placements before entering TCFP.

RT-8. The more likely it was that the child's response to threat was running away, the greater was the number of placements before entering TCFP.

PH-24. The more likely it was that the child had one or more placement(s) in institution(s), the greater was the number of placements before entering TCFP.

Two themes are apparent here. Alcohol problems and running away were associated with a large number of early foster placements. Alochol abuse by the father or in the family generally appears to have had a disruptive influence that extended to the child's foster placements. It is not clear whether the difficulty was that the child's equilibrium was so disturbed as to preclude adjustment to a foster placement, or whether the alcoholic problems in the family were episodic, with the child being retrieved from foster placements by the parents between acute alcoholic episodes.

Running away is, of course, the most self-limiting form of behavior with respect to foster placements. Not only does it stop a placement in the most definite way, it often makes the resumption of a foster placement impossible both emotionally and/or practically.

Poor placements, those that are possible but have many disadvantages, carry their own obvious risk for future placements. Once a child has been placed in a difficult foster placement, his or her expectations for the future begin to assume a negative cast and shape the child's behavior in maladaptive ways. Similarly, an institutional placement carries with it great risk for future placements. As noted previously, there is a chicken-and-egg problem here, but institutional placement cannot provide a good model for a child who is subsequently placed in foster care.

Finally, we again see the importance of the biological father's influence on foster placements. A father who was absent due to death, disease, or incapacity was associated with a child's having a larger number of foster placements. We have no way of knowing from our data whether one component of the father's absence is more harmful than others, but it is unquestionable that as a physical and/or symbolic entity his presence contributes something to his child that makes foster care more stable and secure.

6

Study II Cross-Validation in the Idaho Division

Rationale

The values of R^2 were consistently high for the outcome measures used in the Montana Division study. On the one hand, this result was not unexpected, given the great amount and variety of independent information available for the children in our sample. On the other hand, it made us cautious because regression analysis in general, and stepping procedures especially, capitalize on chance variations within a given sample to produce as large an R^2 as possible. In this sample, for instance, the biological father's having had a criminal record was significantly related to higher levels of the child's present overall global level of functioning. It was not included in the regression equation, but, having survived the first stage of the selection process, it was a candidate for inclusion. Had it been incorporated into the equation, it would have been on the basis that, of the five children whose fathers had a criminal record, three were functioning at a relatively high level and the other two were about average, while of the 46 children whose fathers had no record, about as many were functioning well as were functioning poorly. There was no general relationship between the child's level of functioning and his or her father's having had a criminal record; an accident of the particular sample of children we were working with made it appear that there was until we looked into the matter more closely. The bottom line, although we avoided it in this instance, is that sampling variation can be a major problem in regression analysis.

Let us note that the 51 children from the Montana Division are a sample of the population of all the children it has served and will serve. They are not a random sample, as strict adherence to the statistical model requires, which serves to weaken our inferences somewhat. We limit the period of service that defines the population to a time span over which the mode of operation is basically similar, and services to foster children—and the kind of foster children served—are comparable.

Extreme sampling variation is more common in smaller samples: had we had a sample of 100 children available to us in the Montana Division, ten of whose fathers had criminal records, we might have run into the same problem we encountered there. But it seems more likely that half of the ten children would have been functioning better and the other half worse, assuming, of course, that overall level of functioning is unrelated to the father's having had a criminal record. We used a shrinkage formula to try to take effects due to sampling variation into account, but experience has shown that R^2 will generally decline more in a replication with a new sample, "cross-validation," than the shrinkage formula would indicate.

Given the high values of R^2 achieved in Study I and the very real possibility that the statistical procedures had capitalized on chance variation in the Montana Division sample to produce such large values, we felt that a cross-validation with a similar sample of children was necessary if we were to achieve an accurate idea of the predictive power of the regression models. The immediate question was where to locate a similar sample of children served by The Casey Family Program.

The Idaho Division

A brief set of comparisons convinced us that the Idaho Division of TCFP was the appropriate place for a cross-validation. It was comparable in size, age, management, and setting to the Montana Division. Its director and professional staff were interested in the study and in a position to provide the support, cooperation, and financial backing to complete it.

One of the attractive aspects of a cross-validation sample from the Idaho Division was its similarity in terms of a Rocky Mountain West subculture and urban-rural mix to the overall situation in Montana. Although the samples were similar in most respects, there were differences that deserve comment.

The Idaho Sample

Because of the large degree of similarity between the 55 children in the Idaho Division sample and the 51 from the Montana Division, we limit our description to some basic demographics from Domain II and those characteristics from the other domains on which the two groups differed substantially. For the sake of quick comparisons involving percentages, we use the convention of putting values from Montana in parentheses following those for Idaho.

With respect to demographic characteristics, 62 percent (compared to 59 percent in Montana) of the Idaho Division children were males and 38 percent (compared to 41 percent in Montana) were females. Their average age was almost exactly 17 years, three years older than their Montana counterparts—one of the greatest differences between the two groups. Fourteen percent (vs. 16 percent) were from six to ten years old, 27 percent (vs. 49 percent) were 11 to 15, and 59 percent (vs. 35 percent) were 16 or older. Fewer of the Idaho children were in the 11–15 age group and more were 16 or older.

In terms of racial background, 80 percent (vs. 63 percent) were identified as Caucasian, 4 percent (vs. 6 percent) were Native American, 5 percent (vs. 18 percent) were mixed Native American and other race(s), and 11 percent (vs. 13 percent) belonged to other races, other racial combinations, or were of unknown racial background. There were more white children in the Idaho sample and fewer of mixed Native American ancestry.

Two percent (vs. 26 percent) of the young people were identified as Catholic, 18 percent (vs. 6 percent) were Mormons, 18 percent (vs. 16 percent) were affiliated with other Protestant denominations, and 62 percent (vs. 52 percent) were either members of non-Christian faiths, or, most often, did not have a religious affiliation. The differences in proportions of Catholics and Mormons accounted for most of the differences in religious affiliation between the two groups.

There were 23 other variables in five other domains on which there were substantial differences between the children of the Montana and

Idaho divisions. We will look at Domain I first. With respect to personal characteristics of the foster child, Idaho Division children were more likely to be rated as manipulative and as curious or inquisitive, and less likely to be rated as fearful of intimacy, than children in the Montana Division.

With respect to Domain IV, several differences in family history were apparent. The parents of Idaho Division children had been less frequently divorced—24 percent (vs. 41 percent). The mother more frequently had no contact with her child—58 percent (vs. 29 percent), but less frequently had a history of alcohol abuse, mental illness, or suicide—25 percent (vs. 45 percent). She less frequently lived in the state—31 percent (vs. 51 percent). The father was more frequently deceased—25 percent (vs. 12 percent), but he had much less often failed to accept the child, rejected the child, or had no relationship with the child—4 percent (vs. 31 percent). He more frequently lived in the state—78 percent (vs. 24 percent). Finally, Idaho Division children much less frequently had important relatives other than parents or siblings involved in their lives—22 percent (vs. 60 percent).

The Idaho and Montana children differed in several ways with respect to placement history, Domain VI. Considerably fewer Idaho Division children had been in a foster placement before the present one—20 percent (vs. 41 percent). They were older at first placement—nine years versus six years in Montana—and many fewer had a first placement outside the own home at five years of age or earlier. And where Idaho children suffered placement breakdowns in foster placements outside the own home subsequent to the first, there were only two common risk factors—rejection by the foster family and the nature of the placements themselves—rather than seven as in Montana.

With respect to present placement situation (Domain VII), 55 percent of the Idaho Division children were in foster care at the time of the study (vs. 76 percent). Ten percent more Idaho children were away from home in an educational setting through the Scholarship Program, and 7 percent more were in group homes. Idaho children entered TCFP at a somewhat later age—12.7 years versus 10.7 in Montana. There was a greater tendency to live in another part of the state from their natural parents and to be in more affluent middle-class circumstances than their peers in Montana.

With respect to the characteristics of the present foster family (Domain VIII), Idaho Division foster parents were better educated and were more likely to have a formal religious commitment. A feeling of closeness to young people was more likely to have motivated them to take a foster child into their home, and the mother was less likely to be in the process of liberation.

TERI

Teri is a small, blonde, six-year-old who, with her sister, came into The Casey Family Program six months ago. They were placed with a foster family that has three other Casey children, as well as five of their own children.

Teri's father deserted the family when she was a year old. Her mother has periods of mental instability and, in fact, is never in complete contact with reality; her condition deteriorated when Teri was five, and the sisters were placed in a large state-run children's home. During her stay there, Teri began to show signs of withdrawal and loss of concentration. When Teri and her sister were taken on by TCFP, it was with the expectation that her ten-year-old sister would benefit from a stable, well-disciplined household. It was hoped that Teri might improve somewhat.

The foster family has been taking Casey children for several years and has had some real successes. The family is close and loving, but, because of the number of children involved, there are also some characteristics of a good group home. There is a deep commitment to Christianity, but no one waits for the Lord to provide. Each child has chores and is expected to perform them. The foster mother functions as household executive, but she is also involved with the emotional, intellectual, and spiritual development of each child. The foster father is also interested in and involved with the children.

Teri has bloomed in this household. The family has enough land to keep horses, and Teri has turned out to be an enthusiastic and talented rider. Her coordination, previously poor, is now quite good. Thought to be a marginal learner, she is starting to read, though slowly, and she is very proud of her achievement. And from being restricted emotionally, she is becoming affectionate and responsive. There are still many behavioral problems to be worked on, but there is realistic hope that Teri will grow up to lead a normal life.

In terms of outcome variables, 45 percent of the Idaho Division children had been through one or more placement breakdowns or changes (vs. 27 percent). The ratings on a nine-point scale of overall functioning of the foster child were higher in Idaho, however: 6.16 versus 4.57 in Montana.

Mechanics of Cross-Validation and the Results

To understand the cross-validation process, one should first recall how R^2 was obtained in the original sample. We can think of the multiple regression procedure as essentially doing two things. First it finds the weights to apply to a set of predictors that allow one to reproduce the outcome variable as closely as possible. (The stepwise part of the procedure assures one that a "best" subset of predictors has been chosen.) In the second step, the multiple correlation coefficient, R, is computed between the outcome variable and the weighted combination of predictors. As explained previously, generally we then square R to find the amount of variance in the outcome variable that we can account for with the set of weighted predictors.

In cross-validation, the weights obtained for the set of predictor variables selected in the original sample are applied to the scores on the same set of variables in the cross-validation sample.[7] A weighted sum of predictor variables is calculated, and R is computed between the outcome variable and the weighted sum of predictors. R^2 is then found in order to determine how much of the variance in the outcome variable can be accounted for. This cross-validation procedure has the advantage that the predictors have not been chosen subject to the vagaries of fortuitous accidents attendant on the selection of a particular sample. The values of R^2 from the original Montana Division sample and the cross-validation sample are presented in Table 21.

Discussion

The greatest reduction in R^2 from original sample to cross-validation sample was for the number of placement breakdowns or changes. The shrinkage in this crucial variable was dramatic—from .77 to .30—a greater than 50 percent reduction in predictive power as measured by variance accounted for. Within the context of hit rates, however, the change is not so great. By choosing the cutting points with care,[a] we were able to classify correctly 88 percent of the children in the Montana sample as having had 0, 1, or 2 placement breakdowns or changes. By using the same cutting points, we were able correctly to classify 64 percent of the children in the Idaho sample. Because the proportions of children with 0, 1, or 2 breakdowns were different in Idaho than they were in Montana, we put ourselves at something of a disadvantage by using the same cutting points rather than adjusted ones, but we wished to take a conservative approach to evaluating our statistical model. How good is a 64 percent hit rate? It is, first of all, highly significant ($F = 8.00$, $df = 6, 48$, $p < .01$); that is, it represents a conclusion that is unlikely to be due to chance. It allowed us to classify correctly nearly two-thirds of the Idaho children, 10 percent more than we could have done using a base rate prediction,

[a] As statistically knowledgeable readers will be aware, using multiple regression for an outcome variable with these values and finding cutting points to classify "hits" is similar to employing discriminant function analysis. We employed regression analysis because we considered number of placement breakdowns or changes to have metric rather than purely classificatory properties.

TABLE 21

*Values of R^2 for Outcome Variables in the Original
and Cross-Validation Samples*

Outcome Variable	Montana		Idaho
Placement breakdown	.77	(.74)*	.30
Child's level of functioning	.72	(.65)	.55
Family's level of functioning	.86	(.84)	.58
Choose family again	.86	(.84)	.56

*The value in parentheses is the shrunken value.

including all of those children who had more than a single placement
breakdown or change. As well as allowing pinpointing of those children
most at risk, the statistical model allows us to work with the knowledge of
those factors associated with children in danger of placement breakdown
and offers the possibility of distributing resources in such a way as to
maximize the results of our efforts.

The two level-of-functioning outcome variables and the caseworker's
willingness to choose the foster family again held up well, and more or
less equally, under cross-validation. Our ability to specify factors related
to the functioning of the foster child and the foster family appears to be a
robust one. Part of the reason for the higher R^2's for these outcome
variables is the fact that they have a greater range of possible values
offering greater opportunity to distinguish among individual cases. The
other reason is that these outcomes are based on ratings that share more
with other ratings than can a measure such as number of placement
breakdowns or changes. Such "method variance"[8] is an unavoidable aspect of measurement and does not necessarily represent a serious draw-
back.

Before leaving this material, we should make clear that our work in
the Idaho Division did not encompass only a cross-validation. Using the
same regression techniques as in Montana, we found the best subsets of
predictor variables for each outcome measure. Although there were some
differences between the sets of predictors found to be most useful in the
Idaho and Montana divisions, as would be expected due simply to sampling variation, there was a considerable degree of overlap between them.
The most striking difference between the two sets of results was that all of
the R^2's were higher in the Idaho Division. This appeared to be caused
principally by the greater degree of variability with respect to all of the
outcome variables among Idaho Division foster children and foster fam-

ilies. In general, greater variability offers greater opportunities for predictive accuracy.

We did not, as is sometimes done in similar studies, attempt a reciprocal cross-validation from Idaho to Montana. We have no quarrel with the logic of this procedure, but in this instance it might have been viewed as a means of lending spurious weight to our conclusions.

7

Study III   The Observational Study

Purpose and Rationale

The basic purpose in undertaking the research described in this book was to determine whether placement maintenance was a predictable aspect of foster care; that is, one that could be foretold with some accuracy. A substantial problem associated with the study in Montana and its sequel in Idaho was that the primary outcome variable, number of placement breakdowns or changes, was already known as we gathered our predictor data and computed our regression equation. We were engaged, not in actually foretelling future breakdowns, but in finding factors that were systematically associated with outcomes already known. Although we have no reason to believe that the nature of the breakdown process has changed since the data from the two original samples was gathered, or even since the Montana Division of TCFP began operations, it must be remembered that the proof of the pudding is still in the eating. Until the models that have been developed are proven in foretelling future break-downs and changes, their utility must remain in doubt.

A more pressing problem with the research is that, while some of the most useful predictor variables were items of fact, many others were based on retrospective judgments of child and family characteristics. The reliability of these judgments may have depended upon caseworkers having known and observed the child and his or her foster family for a relatively long period of time. Because this matter was crucial to the use of our regression equations for predictive purposes with children and foster families new to the Program—those people who were the ultimate focus of the research—we embarked on a third study. Its purpose was to discover the extent to which assessments of predictor variables based upon observations of relatively brief samples of foster child and foster family behavior by raters without previous knowledge of child and family characteristics could be shown to be related to placement outcomes.

In many ways it would have been ideal if we could have worked in this third study with a sample of children and foster families new to the Program. But, given the relatively deliberate rate at which children are accepted into the Program, the time (and care) that goes into selecting foster families, and, most of all, the time it takes for an appreciable number of placement breakdowns to occur, this option was not feasible.

Let us repeat that this study was not meant to answer the question of actual predictive use of the equations; that is a matter upon which the jury is still out, although some data relevant to it have been gathered. In this study we were still using outcome data already in hand.

Selection of Variables

Many of the variables investigated in the third study were from the domains of the Montana and Idaho studies. We were, of course, especially interested in those predictors based on ratings and judgments that were substantially related to outcome measures in those studies. But many additional variables were also included. Some of these came directly from the research; that is, they were suggested by earlier findings or grew out of incidental observations as we gathered or analyzed data. Other variables were derived from matters of theoretical interest in the child welfare literature or practical matters related to caseworkers' everyday duties. A few were contributed by interested colleagues who were aware of the research. We shall, for the most part, not make these distinctions in describing the variables, because (1) they have little relevance to our primary purpose of determining the feasibility of obtaining reliable data quickly and simply enough to make the predictive use of the statistical models feasible, and (2) they were generally unrelated to the results of the study.

Predictor Variables in the Third Study

We examined two classes of predictor variables in the third study: direct observations and summary ratings based upon entire periods of observation. We placed observers who knew neither the child nor the foster family in a sample of foster homes for brief periods to gather this information.

Direct Observations

Because of physical limitations on how much an observer can see and record in a naturalistic setting such as a foster home, we decided to concentrate his or her efforts on the public behavior of the person of greatest concern, the foster child. The observer's primary task was to record the frequency of occurrence of certain of the child's manifest behaviors.

The behaviors of the foster child targeted for direct observation are listed in Table 22. They represent ten categories of activities of the foster child which, in the experience of Montana and Idaho division caseworkers, were directly related to long-term adjustment of the child to the foster family environment and therefore to placement maintenance. In addition, pilot work provided some assurance that they would occur with high enough frequency to be observable during a relatively brief time period.

Nine classes of behavior favored long-term adjustment and one was maladaptive. The nine favorable classes are as follows:

1. Seeking attention and assistance from adults. In its highly developed form, this is a superchild behavior, and some degree of it appears to be a necessity in areas as diverse as attaching and problem solving.

2. Making positive self-references. This was considered the most reliable indicator of sufficient self-esteem for the child to have a chance of making a healthy adjustment.

3. Having a hobby or similar interest, especially an athletic or musical one. This was a frequent concomitant of placement maintenance in our earlier studies, and we wished to follow it up within an observational framework.

4. Being able to take scolding, correction, and punishment. Children who were able to take correction without either undue submissiveness or excessive rancor seemed much more often to make successful placements.

5. Being able to handle stress.   We were looking for the ability to be both properly aware of stress and also to react to it constructively.

6. Possessing problem-solving ability.   Three components were important: being able to formulate a solution to a problem, being able to overcome a lack of resources in pursuing a solution, and the ability to make plans and schedules (in an age-appropriate fashion) for the implementation of the solution.

7. Possessing, developing, and using social skills.   Children who were able to give socially skilled responses, especially to their foster parents and their children, appeared to be more likely to make successful long-term adjustments.

8. Possessing some facility in expressing emotions.   The ability to express both positive emotions, such as happiness, and negative ones, such as anger, was regarded as a marker of the child who was able to make use of the positive aspects of life experience and of the foster home in particular.

9. Expressing religious values.   We regarded the expression of religious values as a possible indicator of children who could call up assistance from outside themselves to deal with stress and feelings of depression and hopelessness.

The tenth class included a variety of maladaptive behaviors, but emphasized passive-aggressive responses. We also looked for negative and consistently oppositional behaviors, overcompliance, withholding, lack of empathy for the foster parents, self-pity, disobedience and resistance, open hostility, and verbal aggressiveness.

The abbreviation "DO" is used for the "directly observable" behaviors in this domain. Where appropriate, domain designations from Chapter 2 are given in parentheses at the end of each item.

Summary Ratings

We reasoned that being continuously in the vicinity of the foster child and often near one or both foster parents and their own children would also provide the observer with information about specific aspects of the members of the foster family and about more general and/or more abstract characteristics of the foster child and foster family. So a second task was the rating as a summary of impressions at the end of observation on a given day of another set of variables covering the child, the foster mother, the foster father, and the foster family as a functioning unit.

The items that were to be rated as a summary of impressions at the end of each day's observations are listed in Table 23. Some could have

SUSAN

Susan is a 14-year-old with strawberry blonde hair and a generally sweet expression. She and her nine-year-old half-brother were placed with their Casey foster family a year ago.

Susan spent her first six years living with her mother and a series of her mother's male companions. When she was five, her mother had a second child. When Susan was six, their mother began to leave the children with relatives for longer and longer periods, and she also began to drink heavily. Their grandmother kept them for a two-year period beginning when Susan was nine, and from that time on they almost never saw their mother. When Susan was 11, two of their mother's sisters alternated in giving the children a home, but a year later the aunt who had been the principal caregiver married and was no longer willing to continue. The state took over care of the children, and they were placed, usually separately, in a series of foster homes. When TCFP agreed to take them, the decision was made to place them together in hopes that it would benefit them.

Susan has a pretty face and cultivated an ingratiating manner during her years of being cared for by people who did not really want her. She also developed a facile ability to lie and a determination to do whatever she wanted. In the years when no one was paying much attention to her, that was easy to do.

The children's foster family lives in a very small town close to a larger city. They have a garden and a few animals, and are devoted churchgoers. They have two children, both older than Susan, and one still at home.

The children of this foster family have found it very difficult to accept Susan and her brother. They resent the time and attention that is given them and, in fact, the younger child has got into some uncharacteristic academic and personal trouble since the foster children arrived; however, a TCFP caseworker is counseling the foster parents and their child, as well as Susan and her brother, trying to get the family functioning well as a unit. The foster parents feel they are becoming better parents for their own children as well as for Susan and her brother because of this help.

Susan is very interested in clothes, makeup, and being part of a group. Her foster mother is quite strict as far as having Susan report her whereabouts, do chores, and control her temper, but she also encourages Susan's artistic talent and gives her considerable latitude concerning clothes and room decoration. Susan is becoming more trustworthy and, though she often has temper tantrums, they are becoming fewer. She recognizes that the stability she now has is going to make a great deal of difference to her life and feels it is probably worth the greater restrictions.

TABLE 22

Directly Observable Behaviors of the Foster Child (DO)

Seeks Attention and Assistance
1. Child engages in positive attention-seeking behavior (e.g., engages attention of foster father to get him to sit down, talk to him or her for a moment, not by nagging, whining, or manipulative behavior). (RF-21)
2. Child elicits help or assistance from an adult in a positive way (e.g., gets foster father's help in repairing bike, not by nagging, whining, or manipulative behavior). (RF-21)
3. Child engages in inappropriate but not necessarily maladaptive attention-seeking behaviors (e.g., nagging or whining). (RT-14)
Makes Positive Self-Reference
4. Child makes positive self-reference (e.g., "I am a good person")
Has a Hobby or Similar Interest
5. Child expresses strong interest in and/or engages in activity/hobby/field of study. (PC-19, PC-24, PC-25)
Accepts Correction, Scolding, Punishment
6. Child reacts appropriately to scolding or punishment that is suitable to age and stage of development.
7. Child recovers appropriately from scolding or punishment that is suitable to age and stage of development.
Handles Stress
8. Child is aware of stressful event in his or her environment and reacts appropriately to it (e.g., reports problem that needs attention; helps out when foster parents are trying to get started on trip; moves out of the way when foster parents are battling).
Engages in Problem Solving
9. Child formulates solution to problems in household/playground/activity setting.
10. Child overcomes lack of resources in solving a problem or achieving a goal or finishing a project.
11. Child formulates own plans or schedule for age- and stage-appropriate project/activity/trip/outing (that the family is aware of and is not in conflict with foster family plan or schedule).
Exhibits Social Skills
12. Child makes socially skilled response to social situation involving foster parent(s)/other adult(s)/foster sibling(s)/other children (e.g., is at ease in family gathering, facilitates or initiates an activity). (PC-15)
13. Child interacts appropriately with foster sibling(s) and/or peer(s) (e.g., in play is appropriately assertive rather than aggressive, plays cooperatively, is leader or follower as occasion demands, resolves difficulties without fighting). (PC-15)
14. Child calls foster parent "mom"/"dad"/"first name," rather than "hey, you." (PC-15)

TABLE 22—Continued

Expresses Emotions

15. Child expresses anger appropriately. (RT-7)
16. Child expresses sadness appropriately.
17. Child expresses age-appropriate heterosexual behavior.
18. Child is obviously enjoying himself or herself and/or displays sense of humor.

Expresses Religious Values

19. Child expresses religious values or takes part in a religious practice.

Exhibits Passive-Aggressive or Other Maladaptive Behavior

20. Child engages in (initiating, not reactive) passive-aggressive behavior. (PC-2, RT-2)
21. Child gives a negative response to praise for success or good behavior. (PC-2, RT-2)
22. Child emits more than one opposing or contradicting response in an ongoing sequence of behavior. (PC-2, RT-2)
23. Child is overcompliant. (PC-2, RT-2)
24. Child engages in withholding response (e.g., won't say "yes" when it is called for, or uses many "maybes," or will not commit himself or herself). (PC-2, RT-2)
25. Child invites victimization (e.g., annoys foster parents but cries "foul!" when they retaliate).
26. Child displays lack of empathy for foster parents (e.g., the child is not discriminating about when to ask foster parent for a favor).
27. Child engages in self-pitying, martyred behavior. (RT-18)
28. Child engages in threatening or violent behavior. (RT-1)
29. Child is disobedient or resistant. (RT-3)
30. Child makes hostile response. (RT-7)
31. Child is verbally aggressive. (RT-1)

been directly observed had our priorities been different, but others would have been difficult to translate unambiguously into behavioral terms. Some of both kinds were thought likely to occur with too low a frequency to be reliably observable during a relatively brief assessment period. Others were internal variables of a cognitive or emotional variety, the existence and strength of which had to be inferred through the patterning of other observed and unobserved behaviors.

There were six aspects of the foster mother and her behavior whose ratability on the basis of a brief observational period we wished to investigate. We wanted to see if the consistently predictive emotional coherence and earth mother style could be reliably evaluated over a short time. We were also interested in evidence of compulsivity, which TCFP caseworkers had found to be strongly negatively associated with good placement outcomes. The foster mother's activity level, as an indicator of her capacity to deal with the demands of foster care; her emotional responsiveness to the foster child, as a marker of bonding; and whether or not she was in the process of liberation, as evidence that she might be distancing herself from her family and its needs, were also of interest.

The foster father's emotional involvement with the child and the strength of the male role model he presented were predictors of outcome measures from our earlier studies whose ratability we wished to evaluate. For the same reasons as those concerning the foster mother, we were interested in his activity level and whether he was in the midst of a mid-life reassessment. Whether or not he engaged in activities with the foster child we took to be an indirect indicator of his emotional investment in the foster child.

At the time the third study began, Montana Division caseworkers were formulating a classification of the mechanisms by which the child tried to control foster family members or relationships with them. Many of these mechanisms appeared to be especially maladaptive and indicative of poor placement outcomes. There were nine of importance whose ratability we wished to evaluate: superficial compliance, anger or hostility, self-destructive behavior, attention-seeking behavior, disobedience or resistance, passive-aggressive behavior, oppositional behavior, distancing, and conversational strategies. It should be emphasized that several of these behaviors were also examined in other contexts; here, we focused on their use as control mechanisms.

Because of their utility as predictors in our earlier studies, or in some cases simply because of our desire to determine whether certain descriptions of children commonly used by TCFP caseworkers could be related to placement outcome on the basis of brief observation, we investigated 17 descriptors of the foster child. As an example of the second category, we wished to determine whether a child's "seductiveness," that is, his or her seeming to promise self-revelation in return for attention and social interaction, was a concept for which there were behaviors that observers could reliably identify. The other foster child characteristics we examined were charming and/or expressive, moody or withdrawn, manipulative, dressed and groomed neatly, poor impulse control, low frustration tolerance, low self-esteem, extremely needy of affection, unable to deal with authority, anxious or fearful, untrustworthy, prone to self-destructive behavior, bright/intelligent, emotionally open, always in trouble, and unable to deal with success.

There were 21 aspects of the foster family we examined. These included the predictors of placement outcome from Chapter 5, such as a smothering climate in the foster home and competition between the foster parents for the child's affection; also see items 41, 42, 49, 50, 51, 52, 54, 55, 56, and 60 in Table 23.

In addition, we looked at the degree to which the foster family projected a feeling of genuineness about itself, its style of solving problems and dealing with stress, the goal-directedness of its lifestyle, the degree to which it functioned as a unit, the openness and accepting quality of its attitude toward the child, the niche it provided for the foster child, and its ability to use community and agency support systems.

Finally, in part because our outcome measures of the child's overall level of functioning and the caseworker's willingness to choose the foster family again were from a year to 18 months old and perhaps somewhat out of date at the time of the third study, and in part because of our interest in the relation of global ratings to our outcome measures, we obtained four global ratings from our observers. They were ratings of (1) the degree to which there was a good match between the foster child and the foster family; (2) the degree to which the foster placement generated more pain than pleasure for the foster parents; (3) the child's overall, global level of functioning; and (4) the foster family's overall, global level of functioning. We have used the abbreviation "SR" for this domain. Domain designations from Chapter 2, where appropriate, are given in parentheses at the end of each item.

To recapitulate briefly, variables in the first category were to be observed, recorded, and tallied as they occurred by an observer of a foster child's manifest behavior. Variables in the second category were to be rated as a summary of impressions at the end of observation on a given day and averaged over several such days.

Before beginning formal discussion of matters of experimental design and methodology, our basic strategy should be stated. The observational period should be relatively brief, both for practical purposes, such as manpower, and to avoid intrusion that might deprive a child of privacy or even change the nature of his or her environment adversely. But the period of observation should be long enough to provide a reasonably comprehensive and representative picture of that part of the child's behavioral repertoire that most directly affects his or her adjustment to a foster family and its circumstances.

Experimental Design and Methodology

Sample

The available resources would have allowed observation of 12 to 15 children and their foster families from each of the two divisions; however,

TABLE 23

Daily Summary Ratings (SR)

Foster Mother

1. The foster mother possesses strong emotional coherence. (PF-8)
2. The foster mother has earth mother as her dominant personal style. (PF-9)
3. The foster mother appears to be compulsive as opposed to easygoing with respect to the foster child. (PF-67)
4. The foster mother is emotionally responsive in a positive way to the foster child.
5. The foster mother's activity level is high/moderate/low.
6. The foster mother is in the process of liberation. (PF-6)

Foster Father

7. The foster father provides a strong male role model in the foster family. (PF-16)
8. The foster father is emotionally involved with the child. (PF-17)
9. The foster father engages in activities with the foster child.
10. The foster father's activity level is high/moderate/low.
11. The foster father's behavior indicates a mid-life reassessment.

Foster Child's Control Mechanisms

12. The foster child uses superficial compliance to control foster family members or relationships with them. (RT-18)
13. The foster child uses anger or hostility to control foster family members or relationships with them. (RT-7)
14. The foster child uses withdrawal or moody behavior to control foster family members or relationships with them. (RT-9)
15. The foster child uses self-destructive behavior to control foster family members or relationships with them. (RT-18)
16. The foster child uses attention-seeking behavior to control foster family members or relationships with them. (RT-14)
17. The foster child uses disobedience or resistant behavior to control foster family members or relationships with them. (RT-3)
18. The foster child uses passive-aggressive behavior to control foster family members or relationships with them. (RT-2)
19. The foster child uses oppositional behavior to control foster family members or relationships with them. (RT-18)
20. The foster child uses distancing to control foster family members or relationships with them. (RT-4)
21. The foster child uses other mechanisms *(list includes . . .)* to control foster family members or relationships with them.
22. The foster child talks to foster family members in such a way as to keep them at a distance; that is, uses conversation to control interpersonal distance.

Foster Child Characteristics

23. The foster child is charming and/or expressive. (PC-4)
24. The foster child is moody or withdrawn (age-appropriate). (RT-9)
25. The foster child is manipulative. (PC-7)

TABLE 23—Continued

26. The foster child dresses and grooms neatly. (PC-23)
27. The foster child has poor impulse control. (PC-12)
28. The foster child has a low frustration tolerance. (PC-13)
29. The foster child has low self-esteem. (PC-10)
30. The foster child is extremely needy of affection. (PC-6)
31. The foster child has difficulty in coping with authority. (PH-32)
32. The foster child is anxious or fearful. (PC-9)
33. The foster child is untrustworthy. (PH-34)
34. The foster child engages in self-destructive behavior.
35. The foster child is seductive (by seeming to promise self-revelation in return for attention and social interaction). (PC-18)
36. The foster child is bright/intelligent.
37. The foster child appears to be emotionally open.
38. The foster child is always in trouble.
39. The foster child is unable to deal with success. (PC-11)
Foster Family Characteristics
40. The foster family projects a feeling of genuineness about itself.
41. The foster family manifests an overnurturing or smothering climate in the foster home. (PF-63)
42. The foster family exhibits competition between the foster mother and the foster father for the affection of the child. (PF-64)
43. The foster family is flexible in its ability to solve problems and deal with difficult situations. (PF-33 through PF-39)
44. The foster family's style of dealing with stress is positive; that is, it includes constructive problem solving and analytical approaches. (PF-40)
45. The foster family's style of dealing with stress is passive or negative; that is, to personalize the problem, passively to trust in God to solve the problem, to ignore it and it will go away. (PF-35)
46. The foster parents accept the foster child as he or she is.
47. The foster family's lifestyle can best be described as goal-directed/casual/a combination of the two/neither.
48. The foster family functions emotionally as a unit, including the foster child.
49. The foster family is child-centered. (PF-65)
50. The foster family's ability to handle anger is good. (PF-41)
51. The foster family works through problems to a conclusion. (PF-34)
52. The foster family's ability to share feelings is good. (PF-39)
53. The foster parents have an open and accepting attitude toward the foster child.
54. The foster family has a physically affectionate family style; the child is included in this style, and the inclusion seems natural. The child reciprocates in this style, and the child's reciprocating seems natural (given the length of time the child has been with the foster family). (PF-30)
55. The foster parents exhibit a high degree of comfort in their several roles. (PF-31)
56. The foster parents' personal interaction is one of ease. (PF-32)

TABLE 23—Continued

57. The foster family views itself as a unit, for example, speaks about the "family," tells jokes about the "family," gives each other special status as members of the family.
58. The foster child has a niche in the foster family appropriate to the amount of time he or she has been with them.
59. The foster family uses available support systems, for example, agency, community, church, as part of parenting.
60. One or both foster parents exhibit compulsive behavior. (PF-67)
     Overall Ratings
61. Rating of the degree to which there is a good match between the foster child and the foster family *(plus specific comments)*.
62. Rating of the foster child's overall, global level of functioning.
63. Rating of the foster family's overall, global level of functioning.
64. Rating of the degree to which the foster placement generates more pain than pleasure for the foster parents.

family crises, last-minute changes in vacation plans, foster child summer job requirements, and the like cut the sample down to ten children and their families from the Montana Division and 12 from the Idaho Division. Selection was not random, but was accomplished with the goal in mind of providing a representative range of characteristics (personal, demographic, social, and cultural) of The Casey Family Program young people and families in the two divisions. This strategy could be expected to inflate somewhat the statistical measures of association used to describe relationships in the data. Extreme values of such statistics are also more likely to occur in relatively small samples such as the present one, and a conservative approach to interpreting the results was therefore adopted beforehand. Although the sample was neither random nor large, it was thought to be sufficiently representative to provide reasonable generalizations to the population of children in the two divisions.

Observers

It would have been optimal in terms of experimental design to choose observers as similar to TCFP caseworkers as possible and to equate or counterbalance completely the characteristics of the individuals who were to make the actual observations of the foster children and their families across the two subsamples, but practical considerations of cost, time, and distance prevented this method. Instead, two observers with similar backgrounds in behavioral science and approximately equal overall amounts of experience were chosen. The observer in Idaho was a man in his middle twenties, who had completed one year of a doctoral program in clinical psychology and had managed a number of research projects. The observer in Montana was a woman in her middle forties, who had completed an undergraduate program in psychology as well as several years of graduate work in another field. She had experience as a research associate in many research projects, some of them involving observational techniques. Because the two observers did differ, it was determined that statistical analyses would be done at the end of the data-gathering phase of the study to examine what effects upon the data these dissimilarities might have.

Observational Plan

Because the behavioral and social science literature offered only a few suggestions[9,10,11] as to what might constitute an effective, brief observation period for purposes such as those of this study, the authors drew primarily upon their previous experience in a related area[12] and formulated a goal of 1,000 minutes (16 hours and 40 minutes) of direct observation of each child-family unit, to be spread over a period of four days during a single week. Pilot work indicated that another one to two hours should be added to this base period to compensate for times when the child was engaged in private activities and out of the observer's range. Thus, the observers tried to schedule four to five hours of observation on each of four days with each child-family unit. In general, half of the time was scheduled during an early morning period when child and family were thought to be more likely to be engaged in joint activities that would increase the probability of observing important interactions, and the other half was scheduled for a similar period in the late afternoon or early evening.

At the beginning of the data gathering, three of the four days were scheduled for Monday through Friday, and the other was set up for a weekend day. Data collected through the first half of the study period, however, exhibited no differences between weekday observations and weekend observations. Moreover, data collected over longer time slots during a three-day period (instead of four, to work around the travel plans of two families) displayed the same overall pattern as data collected over four days. Thus, in the second half of the study, data collection was ad lib with respect to weekend days and three- versus four-day periods.

The initial introduction of the observer to the foster child and his or her foster family was accomplished by TCFP caseworker. In general, the caseworker left 15 minutes to an hour after the introduction, and the observer remained a half hour to two hours longer to become better acquainted with the child and the family and to desensitize them somewhat to his or her presence. No observations were made on the day of the introduction, but a tentative schedule for three or four days of observations was worked out or confirmed at this time.

For the most part, arrangements for child-family units to participate in the study had been organized through caseworkers or a division coordinator weeks or months earlier. Family crises, alterations in vacation schedules, and so on, as well as occasional changes of mind about participation, meant that replacement families had occasionally to be recruited on short notice. Resistance to being observed and defensiveness were most likely to occur among these replacement families. On three occasions, such difficulties were appreciable enough to cause the experimenters to discard the data because of probable bias. For the most part, however, the observers encountered only positive or neutral attitudes toward participation in the study.

During the introductory period, the foster child-foster family was informed that the observer wished to be a nonparticipating presence during observation periods and would avoid interaction and conversation. The observers were instructed to avoid attempts to draw them into participation in the life of the family, but not to be rude or abrupt in doing so. They were also told to try to mirror the dominant emotions around them by adopting an appropriate but subdued facial expression. These tactics worked so well that, after the first day with a given child and family, observers reported evoking startle responses from family members who had forgotten their presence and suddenly became aware of it again.

Although unobtrusive, the observers had a definite effect upon both foster child and foster family. Approximately 60 percent of the time, the foster mother or father indicated when asked during an exit interview that the foster child had exhibited better-than-average behavior during the observation period. Comments from the foster children indicated that a similar proportion of the foster parents had also exhibited calmer or more accepting behavior than was usual. Post hoc analysis produced no significant correlations between coded versions of either a foster child or foster parent behavior enhancement variable and any other variable.

Training Program

Before undertaking actual field work, both observers went through a five-day training period to familiarize them thoroughly with the observation procedures and variables and to help them achieve an acceptable degree of reliability with respect to both direct observations and summary judgments. The training was done through the cooperation of a Program family having three Casey foster children (two from the same biological family) as well as several other adoptive and own children.

After three initial one- to two-hour sessions devoted to discussing the behavioral meanings of various items from the assessment instruments and distinguishing among categories of behavior, the two observers were introduced to the training family. The introduction was provided by the caseworker and the first author in much the same fashion in which later introductions would be made. As would also be the usual procedure, the observers were given only a brief, standardized sketch of the foster child and foster family that provided little more than the names and ages of child and family members and the length of time that the foster child had been with the family. The limited amount of introductory information was intended to minimize impression formation by the observer that might bias subsequent observations or judgments. The caseworker and the first author left after about 30 minutes, and the observers remained with the family for an additional hour and a half to become better acquainted and begin to habituate the family to their presence.

On the succeeding four days, the two observers concentrated on a different Casey foster child (but the same one for both observers) during an early and a late period, each lasting one and a half to two and a half hours. After each period, the observers were debriefed, explications of various behavioral categories were given, and reliability coefficients were computed for the behavioral categories given in Table 22. Reliability, computed as the sum of agreements in observing instances of particular behavioral categories divided by the total number of observations of all categories by both observers, reached a value of .70 for the first period. It then dropped to about .60 for the next two days and rose to its initial value of .70 on the final day as a stable consensus was reached on the behavioral meanings of the several items given in Table 22.

To facilitate identification of corresponding observations by the two observers, they were instructed to divide each hour into ten-minute segments, beginning on the hour. They were encouraged to make brief written notes to provide continuity and to record unusual, interesting, or clinically relevant behavior. Where an uninterrupted, ongoing category of behavior spanned two or more ten-minute periods, it was recorded once in each ten-minute interval. In the rare cases where clinically relevant material was recorded, the observers wrote it up in detailed form the evening of the same day and submitted a separate report to the first author. Both observers were instructed about confidentiality requirements with respect to the material, and procedural safeguards to ensure confidentiality were instituted.

At the end of the second observational period during each day, each observer made summary ratings of the items in Table 23. The correlations between these ratings (over the entire set of items), made on a five-point scale with "1" anchoring the positive end of the scale, "3" representing the neutral point, and "5" anchoring the negative end, was above .90 on the first day and stabilized at .95 on the fourth and fifth days of training. Such a degree of inter-rater agreement might seem unusually high, but it should be remembered that it was over the entire set of behaviors. Agreement with respect to individual items was, of course, somewhat lower. The training period did not provide enough data to estimate reliabilities for separate items.

On the last day of training, both observers conducted an exit interview with a different child; an exit interview with the foster mother was also conducted. The exit interviews covered the reactions of the child or foster parent to various aspects of the observational process. They also included a debriefing and several items not pertinent to this research.

As was the usual procedure through the period of the study, care was exercised that all interviews were private and were conducted without the presence of the other party. No material from either interview was ever conveyed to the other party. The interviews were semistructured in that the observers were given the latitude to change the order in which questions were asked, to delete them if the information had already been obtained through observation, or to reword them as appropriate to the educational, social, or cultural circumstances of the interviewee. Care was taken in the debriefing to ensure that both observers were aware of and in agreement with respect to the information to be shared with the child and foster parents.

Observational Period

The period during which observations were undertaken spanned the summer vacation period of the Montana Division children. Observation of Idaho division children began one week later than in Montana and, due to scheduling problems, stretched three weeks into the fall school term. The pattern of data from children observed during the school term appeared essentially identical to that of the others from both divisions.

Results

Methodological Results

Twenty-two foster children and their foster families were observed during the study period. Three of these were eliminated because of excessively defensive behavior. The most usual instances of such behavior were failure by the child and/or the family to be at home for scheduled observations and the foster child's purposefully placing himself or herself out of range of observation. Of the 19 child-family units that remained, ten were from the Montana Division and nine were from the Idaho division. The rate of attrition was within the anticipated 10 to 15 percent limits.

On the average, each foster child was observed for 930 minutes with a standard deviation of 155 minutes. (To oversimplify somewhat, such a standard deviation implies that two-thirds of the children were observed for periods ranging from 775 to 1,085 minutes, while the other third were observed for periods that were about 155 minutes shorter or longer, respectively. The primary reason for the large standard deviation is that one foster child who provided only 565 usable minutes of observation time was included on the basis that the data were proportionately representative to the aggregate data with respect to the behavioral categories, even though there was some evidence of defensiveness. The mean number of minutes of observation per child was significantly lower in Idaho than in Montana, primarily because of the inclusion of this child and because one Montana child was observed for several extra hours to include an unusual extended family gathering.

Because of attrition among the families originally designated for inclusion in the study and the necessity for ad hoc replacements on short notice, a shift in outcome measures was required. The original research plan involved use of the number of placement breakdowns or changes while in The Casey Family Program as the major dependent variable, with 40 percent to 60 percent having experienced one or more breakdowns or changes. In the final sample, the obtained value was 16 percent, too low for effective differential prediction in a sample size of 19. Several other measures were examined as possible replacements: *(1)* total number of placement breakdowns or changes before entering TCFP, *(2)* total number of placement breakdowns or changes before and since entering TCFP, and *(3)* length of time in present foster placement. In terms of desirable psychometric properties, including a mean value that is not too extreme, a reasonable amount of variability, and a fairly symmetrical distribution, the best outcome measure was total number of placement breakdowns or changes before and since entering TCFP, and it became our primary outcome measure.

We had also planned to use the three other outcome measures employed in the Montana and Idaho studies (the caseworker's rating of the foster child's overall functioning, of the foster family's overall functioning, and of his or her willingness to choose the foster family again), but, unfortunately, the overall foster family functioning measure had too little variability to be useful in a correlational analysis, and it was not employed in this study. Briefly, it appears that the families that we were able to schedule for summer observational periods were clustered fairly close together at levels slightly above the means for the respective states. Families who were doing "a little better than OK" seem to have been most amenable to participating in the study.

As noted above, the inter-rater reliability over the set of behavioral categories was .70; over the set of summary ratings it was .95. Conservative methodological practice would have required the reassessment of these values later in the period of study to ensure that they had not fallen below acceptable levels. Although this was the authors' original plan, practical difficulties, especially overlapping schedules of the two observers, prevented this desirable alternative. As evidence of the continued agreement between the two observers, however, several facts should be noted. The rates (per minute) over the entire summer at which the two observers recorded responses were .213 (Montana) and .221 (Idaho). The mean overall numbers of behavioral categories in which observations were recorded for a given child were 15.8 (Montana) and 18.1 (Idaho). The mean numbers of negative behavioral categories in which observations were recorded for a given child were 3.0 (Montana) and 4.0 (Idaho). Not only are these values very close, but none of the differences even approaches significance at the usual level. The only statistically significant difference between the two observers was in the mean frequency with which DO-13 in Table 22, "Child interacts appropriately with foster sibling(s) and/or peer(s)," was recorded. The mean level in Montana, 69.8, was very much higher than the value in Idaho, 16.6. This mean difference appears to be due, however, not to biases in observers but to differences in the mean numbers of foster siblings in the families in the two divisions. The average was 3.4 in Montana and only 1.6 in Idaho. Given the considerably greater opportunities for interaction among the foster children in the Montana Division families, the mean difference would appear to be a function of different family composition rather than of biases between observers.

It could, of course, be argued that, because in the experimental design sense observers and divisions of The Casey Family program were completely confounded, the lack of significant differences is as good evidence for the overall similarity of the two subsamples of foster children-foster families as it is for interobserver reliability. The two possibilities cannot be completely disentangled in this situation, but substantial differences either in observers or in foster children-foster families should have led to substantial and significant differences in mean frequencies or mean ratings. Without unduly stretching the point, the lack of such differences would appear to imply both similarity between the two divisional subsamples *and* similarity between the frames of reference and recording practices of the two observers. Based upon the original reliability estimates and these arguments, it will be assumed that the data of the study are sufficiently reliable to warrant the interpretations in succeeding sections.

It was anticipated that some of the independent variables included in Tables 22 and 23 would, because of their low frequency of occurrence within relatively limited time periods, possess insufficient variability to warrant their retention beyond the initial data analysis. Variables with small variances are seldom useful as predictors and may, if their distributions are skewed, artifactually produce findings that apparently contradict findings based on psychometrically more desirable predictors. Thus, several predictor variables were eliminated because of too little variability. That is, their means may have been high, medium, or low, but most children displayed much the same value. In fact, most of these variables had low mean levels. This matter will be discussed in more detail below, but it is interesting that slightly more than half of the variables to be directly observed were eliminated, while only five of the summary rating variables were removed.

Substantive Results

The predictors that were substantially related to the outcome measures are listed in Tables 24 through 26. The values of the means and standard deviations of the predictors are given as well as the correlations with outcome variables. Because of the small sample size in the third study, we adopted a more stringent criterion for accepting a correlation as demonstrating a systematic relationship rather than being due to sampling variability. We insisted that the predictor account for at least 20 percent of the variance in the outcome measure. This level required a correlation of approximately |.46|.[a]

It should be noted that the mean of a "direct observation" variable is the average number of times a behavior was seen and recorded over the periods of observation of the 19 children in the sample. The mean of a "summary rating" variable was the average of 19 sets of (usually) four post-second-observation-period ratings, each on a five-point scale of the type described above.

The relationships among the outcome measures were somewhat different from those in the Montana Division study. The number of placement breakdowns had higher correlations with the other two outcomes, as

---

[a] This level represents more than twice as stringent a criterion as the usual .05 level of significance.

TABLE 24

Predictor Variables That Correlated | .46| or More with
Total Numbers of Placement Breakdowns Before and
Since Entering The Casey Family Program

	Variable	Mean	Standard Deviation	Correlation
SR-7	The foster father provides a strong male role model.	2.2	.7	.57*
SR-55	The foster parents exhibit a high degree of comfort in their several roles.	2.3	.7	.54
SR-11	The foster father's behavior indicates a mid-life reassessment.	3.8	.5	−.52
DO-18	Child is obviously enjoying himself/herself and/ or displays sense of humor.	27.9	13.7	−.51
DO-17	Child expresses age-appropriate heterosexual behavior.	4.4	4.7	−.50
SR-40	The foster family projects a feeling of genuineness about itself.	2.3	.7	.57
SR-62	Rating of the foster child's overall level of functioning.	2.4	.7	.49
SR-49	The foster family is child-centered.	2.3	.9	.47

*Correlations involving SR variables may appear at first glance to be reversed due to the anchor points on the rating scale.

would be expected, since the measure included breakdowns and changes before as well as since entering TCFP. The ratings of the child's overall functioning and of the caseworker's willingness to choose the family again were more highly correlated than in the earlier study, due, at least in part, to the decision to choose children who varied over the range represented in the Montana and Idaho divisions.

The mean number of placement breakdowns or changes with the new variable, 3.2, was, of course, higher. It was also much more variable, with a standard deviation of 3.0.

The mean rating of the child's overall level of functioning was 5.7, with a standard deviation of 1.9. Thus, the children in this sample were functioning better, on the average, than those in the initial study, because, again, they were selected to reflect somewhat more accurately the range of children-families in the two divisions.

The mean rating on a nine-point scale of the caseworker's willingness to choose the foster family again was 6.7 (corresponding roughly to a rating of 3.7 on a five-point scale, such as was used in the Montana Division study), with a standard deviation of 1.9. The caseworkers were more

ALICE

Alice is an undersized and immature 16-year-old with a shy, untamed, and remote look about her. She has been with her Casey foster family for three years.

Alice was born on a ranch in Wyoming of a very poor, almost illiterate, fundamentalist Christian family. She was half-starved, beaten, overworked, and brainwashed by both parents and was sexually abused by her father. When she was removed from her parents by the state at the age of 11, she was almost psychotic. She was placed in a series of custodial homes but seemed to have been so badly damaged that, though she did not lose ground, she made no progress. She was accepted by The Casey Family Program when she was 13.

Every few months after Alice was taken from her parents, a letter would arrive from them telling her that she would go to hell for abandoning them and demanding that she return. TCFP decided that a considerable distance between Alice and them might help ease both her fear and guilt, and so a placement was found for her in Montana.

Alice's foster parents are strong individuals who cherish and defend their right to be themselves. They have encouraged Alice in those things she can do, but have not expected her to behave like an emotionally normal child. They do expect that she will control her temper and perform the household chores given her.

Alice behaves more like a ten-year-old than one who is 16. She has a bicycle, and in summer most of her time is spent riding it with a small coeterie of nine- to 12-year-olds. The physical exertion and freedom the bicycle gives her are very important, and she is in much better emotional control of herself at home when she can spend several hours a day riding. The semirural area in which the family lives has ideal space for that.

Alice seems settled, if not at ease. Her conversation is very simple and without much emotional content, but she is doing well at the high school she attends. Both her foster family and her caseworker have guarded hopes that she will eventually be able to lead a productive life.

willing to choose again families whose overall level of functioning was higher.

Number of Placement Breakdowns or Changes

The variables that correlated |.46| or greater with number of placement breakdowns or changes before and since entering TCFP are listed in Table 24. Verbal statements of the relationships are given below. The strongest relationships among predictor variables and placement maintenance are given first, followed by those that accounted for less variance.

SR-7.   The more the foster father was rated as providing a strong male role model in the foster family, the smaller the number of placement breakdowns or changes the child had experienced before and since entering TCFP.

SR-55.   The more the foster parents were rated as exhibiting a high degree of comfort in their several roles, the smaller the number of placement breakdowns or changes the child had experienced before and since entering TCFP.

SR-11.   The more the foster father's behavior was rated as indicating a mid-life reassessment, the larger the number of placement breakdowns or changes the child had experienced before and since entering TCFP.

DO-18.   The more frequently the child was observed to be obviously enjoying himself or herself and/or displaying a sense of humor, the smaller the number of placement breakdowns or changes the child had experienced before and since entering TCFP.

DO-17.   The more frequently the child was observed to be expressing age-appropriate heterosexual behavior, the smaller the number of placement breakdowns or changes the child had experienced before and since entering TCFP.

SR-40.   The more the foster family was rated as projecting a feeling of genuineness about itself, the smaller the number of placement breakdowns or changes the child had experienced before and since entering TCFP.

SR-62.   The higher the observer's rating of the child's overall level of functioning in the present foster home, the smaller the number of placement breakdowns or changes the child had experienced before and since entering TCFP.

SR-49.   The more the foster family was rated as child-centered, the smaller the number of placement breakdowns or changes the child had experienced before and since entering TCFP.

The foster father was obviously a very important factor in placement maintenance. A foster father who provided a strong male role model was associated with fewer breakdowns or changes, while a foster father in the midst of a mid-life reassessment went with more breakdowns.

Three aspects of the foster family were substantially related to placement maintenance: the degree of comfort of the foster parents in their several roles, the child-centeredness of the family, and the degree to which it projected a feeling of genuineness about itself.

Two observational variables were of importance. The degree to which the child was able visibly to enjoy himself or herself and his or her ability to express age-appropriate heterosexual behavior were substantially associated with placement maintenance.

Finally, the observer's rating of the child's overall level of functioning was positively related to placement maintenance. Children whose level of functioning was rated higher had fewer breakdowns or changes; those whose functioning was rated lower had more. Once again, the sequence of cause and effect is unclear. It may be that children whose level of functioning is higher to begin with experience greater success in their foster placements and suffer fewer breakdowns or changes than those whose level of functioning has always been lower. It may also be the situation that children who have experienced less than satisfactory placements, many of which have collapsed around them, come to function less well, while those whose placements have been stable and of high quality have been nurtured to a higher level of overall functioning.

Of the eight variables that correlated |.46| or more with the outcome measure, two were based on direct observations and six were the product of summary ratings.

Child's Overall Level of Functioning

The variables that correlated |.46| or greater with the caseworker's rating of the child's overall, global level of functioning from the earlier studies are listed in Table 25. Verbal statements of the relationships are given below. The strongest relationships between predictor variables and the child's level of functioning are given first, followed by those that accounted for less variance.

It should be noted that, in terms of significant correlations in this study, the caseworker's original rating of the child's overall level of functioning was a better outcome measure than the observer's summary rating of the global functioning variable, SR-62. (The same conclusion held for the caseworker's willingness to choose the foster family again.) It seems apparent that caseworkers were not rating *present* overall, global level of functioning in the Montana and Idaho studies. After-the-fact discussions led the authors to conclude that what was actually rated was a *representative* level of overall functioning.

SR-31.   The more the child was rated as having difficulty coping with authority, the lower had been the caseworker's rating of his or her overall, global level of functioning.

SR-14.   The more the child was rated as using withdrawal or moody behavior to control foster family members or relationships with them, the lower had been the caseworker's rating of his or her overall, global level of functioning.

SR-18.   The more the child was rated as using passive-aggressive behavior to control foster family members or relationships with them, the lower had been the caseworker's rating of his or her overall, global level of functioning.

TABLE 25

Predictor Variables That Correlated |.46| or More with the Caseworker's Rating of the Child's Overall, Global Level of Functioning

	Variable	Mean	Standard Deviation	Correlation
SR-31	The foster child has difficulty coping with authority.	3.2	.8	.67
SR-14	The foster child uses withdrawal or moody behavior to control foster family members or relationships with them.	2.8	.8	.62
SR-18	The foster child uses passive-aggressive behavior to control foster family members or relationships with them.	3.2	.6	.61
SR-25	The foster child is manipulative.	3.0	.8	.57
SR-17	The foster child uses disobedience or resistant behavior to control foster family members or relationships with them.	3.3	.8	.57
DO-18	Child is obviously enjoying himself or herself and/or displays sense of humor.	27.9	13.7	.51
SR-46	The foster parents accept the foster child as he or she is.	2.4	.6	−.51
SR-58	The foster child has a niche in the foster family appropriate to the amount of time he or she has been with them.	2.4	.8	−.51

SR-25. The more the child was rated as manipulative, the lower had been the caseworker's rating of his or her overall, global level of functioning.

SR-17. The more the child was rated as using disobedience or resistant behavior to control foster family members or relationships with them, the lower had been the caseworker's rating of his or her overall, global level of functioning.

DO-18. The more frequently the child was observed to be obviously enjoying himself or herself and/or displaying a sense of humor, the higher had been the caseworker's rating of his or her overall, global level of functioning.

SR-46. The more the foster parents were rated as accepting the foster child as he or she was, the higher had been the caseworker's rating of his or her overall, global level of functioning.

SR-58. The more the foster child was rated as having a niche in the foster family appropriate to the amount of time he or she has been with the family, the higher had been the caseworker's rating of his or her overall, global level of functioning.

It is worthy of note that the five variables most substantially related to the earlier rating of the child's overall, global level of functioning were based on summary ratings. These five all have to do with maladaptive behaviors, and three involve the child's attempts to control foster family members or his or her relationships with them. Inability to cope with authority was strongly associated with a lower overall level of functioning. At only a slightly higher level were the use of withdrawal or moody behavior, or of passive-aggressive behavior, or of disobedience or resistance to control foster family members. Manipulative behavior was also strongly associated with lower levels of overall functioning.

Two summary ratings were less highly, but still substantially, related to the child's overall functioning. The ability of the foster parents to accept the child as he or she was, and the child's having a niche in the foster family appropriate to the amount of time he or she had been with them were associated with higher levels of functioning.

The only directly observed variable that was substantially related to the child's overall level of functioning was his or her ability freely to be seen to enjoy himself or herself or to display a sense of humor.

Willingness to Choose the Foster Family Again

The variables that correlated |.46| or more with the caseworker's rating of his or her willingness to place a child, although not necessarily the same child, with the same foster family if the choice were to be made again on the basis of present knowledge are listed in Table 26. Verbal statements of the relationships are given below. The strongest relationships between predictor variables and the caseworker's willingness to choose the family again are given first, followed by those that accounted for less variance.

SR-18.   The more the child was rated as using passive-aggressive behavior to control foster family members or relationships with them, the less was the willingness of the caseworker to place a child with the same foster family if the choice were to be made again on the basis of present knowledge.

SR-9.   The more the foster father was rated as engaging in activities with the foster child, the greater was the willingness of the caseworker to place a child with the same foster family if the choice were to be made again on the basis of present knowledge.

SR-53.   The more the foster parents were rated as having an open and accepting attitude toward the child, the greater was the willingness of

TABLE 26

Predictor Variables That Correlated | .46| or More with the Caseworker's Rating of His or Her Willingness to Choose the Foster Family Again

	Variable	Mean	Standard Deviation	Correlation
SR-18	The foster child uses passive-aggressive behavior to control foster family members or relationships with them.	3.2	.6	.61
SR-9	The foster father engages in activities with the foster child.	2.7	.8	−.57
SR-53	The foster parents have an open and accepting attitude toward the foster child.	2.4	.8	−.56
SR-58	The foster child has a niche in the foster family appropriate to the amount of time he or she has been with them.	2.4	.8	−.54
SR-64	Rating of the degree to which the foster placement generates more pain than pleasure for the foster parents.	3.6	.8	.53
SR-61	Rating of the degree to which there is a good match between the foster child and the foster family.	2.3	.9	−.50
DO-12	Child makes socially skilled response to social situation involving foster parent(s)/other adult(s)/ foster sibling(s)/other children.	10.9	7.5	.47
SR-52	The foster family's ability to share feelings is good.	2.8	.6	−.46

the caseworker to place a child with the same foster family if the choice were to be made again on the basis of present knowledge.

SR-58.   The more the foster child was rated as having a niche in the foster family appropriate to the amount of time he or she had been with them, the greater was the willingness of the caseworker to place a child with the same foster family if the choice were to be made again on the basis of present knowledge.

SR-64.   The more a foster placement was rated as generating more pain than pleasure for the foster parents, the less was the willingness of the caseworker to place a child with the same foster family if the choice were to be made again on the basis of present knowledge.

SR-61.   The more the match between the child and the foster family was rated a good one, the greater was the willingness of the caseworker to place a child with the same foster family if the choice were to be made again on the basis of present knowledge.

DO-12. The more frequently the child was observed to make a socially skilled response to a social situation involving foster parent(s)/ other adult(s)/foster sibling(s)/other children, the greater was the willingness of the caseworker to place a child with the same foster family if the choice were to be made again on the basis of present knowledge.

SR-52. The more the foster family's ability to share feelings was rated as good, the greater was the willingness of the caseworker to place a child with the same foster family if the choice were to be made again on the basis of present knowledge.

All but one of the eight variables that correlated substantially with the caseworker's willingness to choose the foster family again was based on summary ratings. The strongest relationship reflected the caseworkers' unwillingness to make another placement with foster parents whose foster child used passive-aggressive tactics to control them. Discussion of this relationship with TCFP caseworkers indicated that it was a combination of sympathy for what the family had endured and irritation that the foster parents could not control the behavior.

Caseworkers were strongly inclined to make another placement in a family in which the foster father engaged in activities with the child. Foster families that had a good ability to share their feelings and an open and accepting attitude toward the foster child were favored, as were those in which the child had a niche appropriate to the amount of time he or she had been with the family. Not surprisingly, caseworkers favored foster families in which there appeared to be a good match between child and family and in which the foster placement did *not* generate more pain than pleasure for the parents.

The only directly observed behavior that was substantially related to a willingness to choose a foster family again was the child's tendency to make socially skilled responses in social situations involving the foster family. A family in which such responses occur is highly valued.

Summary

There were three variables that were substantially correlated with more than one outcome measure. Two were summary ratings and one was directly observed. They are listed in Table 27.

Only SR-18, which involves passive-aggressive behavior, had a counterpart among items from the first study. The relationship is not direct, since SR-18 focuses on passive-aggressive tactics for controlling the foster family rather than behavior in general (PC-2), or as a risk factor in foster placements (PH-29), but, nonetheless, the two passive-aggressive items used in the first two studies correlated substantially with outcome variables and entered their respective regression equations. Once again,

TABLE 27

Variables That Correlated |.46| or More With
More Than One Outcome Measure

		Outcome Measure		
	Item	PBD	FOC	CFA
DO-18	Child is obviously enjoying himself or herself and/or displays sense of humor.	+	+	
SR-18	The foster child uses passive-aggressive behavior to control foster family members or relationships with them.		+	+
SR-58	The foster child has a niche in the foster family appropriate to the amount of time he or she has been with them.		+	+

passive-aggressive behavior is one of the least tolerable aspects of foster child behavior.

Two other items that correlated substantially with outcome variables in the third study were among the variables that correlated with two or more outcome variables in the Montana study. SR-49 (PF-65) described the foster family as child-centered, and SR-52 (PF-39) characterized the foster family's ability to share feelings as good.

SR-46, "The foster parents accept the child as he or she is," and SR-53, "The foster parents have an open and accepting attitude toward the foster child," two items that correlated substantially with outcome measures in this study, have much in common with PF-62, "The foster family can tolerate unassimilated aspects of the foster child," which correlated |.35| or more with all four outcome measures in the Montana study and entered three regression equations.

Similarly, SR-9, "The foster father engages in activities with the foster child," has more than a little in common with PF-17, "The foster father is emotionally involved with the child," which correlated |.35| or more with two outcome variables in the Montana study.

In addition, SR-14, dealing with moody and withdrawn behavior, SR-17, dealing with disobedient or resistant behavior, SR-7, which describes the foster father as providing a strong masculine role model, and SR-55, which characterizes the foster parents as exhibiting a high degree of comfort in their several roles, all have counterparts among items that correlated |.35| or more with outcome measures in the Montana study.

In general, the direct observation categories of behavior appear to have limited promise as variables that could be used to predict placement maintenance and success, at least when based upon periods of 15 or 16

hours' duration. Moreover, it seems doubtful that longer periods of observation would improve the utility of these variables to any appreciable
extent, since so many of them had quite low frequencies of occurrence.
Variables 1, 2, 3, 4, 7, 8, 9, 10, 11, 15, 16, 19, 20, 21, 22, 23, 24, 25, 26,
27, 28, 29, 30, and 31 in Table 22 all had mean frequencies of less than 4.0
over the entire observational period. Thus, on the average, these responses were observed less than one time in any four-hour period. Although the remaining eight variables had mean frequencies ranging from
4.2 to 35.8, only three of them exhibited significant correlations with one
or another of a set of selected outcome measures. It is interesting that,
from among these three, the variable with the highest mean frequency of
occurrence concerned the child's obviously enjoying himself or herself or
displaying a sense of humor. The variable with the intermediate mean
value involved making socially skilled responses to adults or other children, and the variable with the lowest mean was the category of age-
appropriate heterosexual behavior. All three direct observation variables
had correlations toward the low end of the range of significant correlations.

Conclusions

The variables that have greatest promise as predictors of placement
maintenance and success based upon short observational periods are
among those listed in Table 23. The data from these variables were
generated by observers' ratings at the end of the second observation
period on any given day. These ratings were highly reliable and tended to
vary but little, over two or three succeeding days, from the values assigned after the first day of observation. In fact, these ratings were
aggregated as the modal value of the three or four daily values for the
purpose of generating correlations, since the mode was a more faithful
representation of the data than was the mean. Predictions based upon a
single day's observations would, of course, tend to have lower correlations
with the dependent measures. Because the reliabilities of these variables
are high, however, the decrease could be expected to be quite small.

The daily summary judgments that appear to have the greatest potential utility for predicting future placement success fall into three categories: (1) maladaptive strategies of the foster child for coping with or
controlling the foster family, (2) characteristics of the foster father, and (3)
positive aspects of the foster family as a family.

On the one hand, as has been demonstrated so clearly in the two
earlier studies, maladaptive strategies such as passive-aggressive behavior
are strong indicators of placement failure. Withdrawal and moodiness,

resistant or disobedient behavior, manipulative tendencies, and trouble in coping with authority all are likely to be potent predictors that a foster child is not a good candidate for a successful placement.

On the other hand, various positive aspects of prospective foster families would predict that placements made with them would be successful. These aspects include the foster parents' comfort in their several roles, their ability to share their feelings, the degree to which they project an impression of genuineness and sincerity, and the degree to which the foster home is child-centered.

Characteristics of the foster father as predictors of placement maintenance and success have also been prominent in the authors' earlier studies. For the present sample, it is important that the foster father present a strong masculine role model, that he engage in activities with the child, and that he *not* be involved in a mid-life reassessment.

In conclusion, then, it appears that accurate predictions of placement success based upon relatively short periods of observation of a foster child, a prospective foster family, and the two together, are feasible. Six to eight hours of observation of the foster child and prospective foster family together might well form a satisfactory data base from which to generate predictions. Whether the predictions would reach the standards of accuracy indicated in the two earlier studies is an empirical question, but, whether they did or not, there is little doubt that such data-based predictions would provide additional useful information to aid the professional staff in making optimal placement decisions.

8

Summary and Conclusions

The Casey Family Program provides a planned, long-term approach to subsidized foster care for the underachievers of the child welfare system. Its concept is a marriage of what foster care professionals know about effectively helping children and what managers know about effectively running organizations.

The purpose of our studies of The Casey Family Program was to determine whether the outcomes of its foster placements were predictable from factors that could be known, at least in principle, at the time the placements were made. We built statistical models of placement maintenance based upon characteristics of (a) the foster child, (b) his or her biological family, and (c) the foster family.

We used two main sources of data to construct our models: archival material on the child and his or her biological family, and caseworker ratings of various aspects of the child and his or her foster family. We used information from a sample of 51 children served by the Montana Division of The Casey Family Program to build our models. These models in general provided quite accurate predictions of placement outcomes. We then cross-validated the models with a sample of 55 children from the Idaho Division. There was a substantial amount of shrinkage in the variance accounted for in the cross-validation sample, but outcomes remained largely predictable.

To determine whether predictions of placement outcomes could be based upon brief assessments of factors that could be evaluated at the time placements were made, we undertook a third study. The results of that study implied that summary ratings of salient characteristics of foster children and foster families based upon as little as a single day's observation could be used to predict placement outcomes effectively.

Several specific aspects of these studies deserve emphasis. First, our research confirmed that the children served by the Montana and Idaho divisions of TCFP were among the underachievers of the child welfare system whom Jim Casey desired to reach. It also confirmed that the Montana and Idaho Divisions were doing an effective job of serving those children. Their placements were generally stable, and both foster children and foster families were rated as functioning at levels that ranged from acceptable to good.

Second, the predictors of various aspects of placement outcomes formed a stable set that emphasized specific aspects of the foster child's history (such as age at first placement and one or more placements in an institution) and maladaptive behaviors (such as passive-aggressive responses), and characteristics of the foster mother (such as her emotional coherence), the foster father (such as the degree of his emotional involvement with the foster child), and the foster home (such as its child-centeredness).

Third, it was possible to combine these characteristics in a multiple regression equation in such a way as to give meaningful weights to their contributions to placement outcome. The shift in outcome measures necessitated in the third study by a restricted range of placement breakdowns raises some questions, but work by Dawes[13] would argue that the equations can be modified simply and effectively to provide accurate predictions of placement outcomes.

Fourth, as we have pointed out previously, our results are based upon information already in hand, and their use for predictive purposes remains to be demonstrated. What data we have support the utility of the statistical models, but we are not yet in a position to make a definitive statement. It is our hope that other workers in the child welfare discipline will help test our conclusions.

Along this line, it should be obvious to the reader that we have raised many more questions than we have provided answers for. This is especially the case with respect to the nature of the causal links between our predictors and our outcome variables. We would have preferred to speculate at greater length on many of these connections, but the correlational nature of our data and its logical limitations made caution desirable. Nonetheless, many of the relationships we have described have substantial implications for foster care, and it is our hope that other investigators will examine them within more rigorous frameworks.

Finally, it may be the case that our results will be shown to be applicable only within the rather special environment currently enjoyed by The Casey Family Program. Should this be so, we hope that the specificity of our results and the testability of hypotheses that that implies will provide impetus for the formation of additional planned, long-term programs of foster care of the kind envisioned and first implemented by Jim Casey.

References

1. Rutter, M. (1978) Early sources of security and competence. In J. Bruner and A. Garton (editors), *Human Growth and Development*. Oxford: Clarendon Press.

2. Garmezy, N. (1976) *Vulnerable and Invulnerable Children: Theory, Research and Intervention*. Master lecture on developmental psychology, American Psychological Association.

3. Murray, H. (1938) *Explorations in Personality*. New York: Oxford.

4. Jackson, D. (1974) *Personality Research Form Manual*. Goshen, NY: Research Psychologists Press.

5. American Psychiatric Association. (1980) *Diagnostic and Statistical Manual of Mental Disorders (DSM-III)* Washington, DC: American Psychiatric Association.

6. Draper, N., and Smith, H. (1981) *Applied Regression Analysis (2nd Edition)*. New York: Wiley.

7. Nunnally, J. (1978) *Psychometric Theory (2nd Edition)*. New York: McGraw-Hill.

8. Campbell, D., and Fiske, D. (1959) Convergent and discriminant validation by the multitrait-multimethod matrix. *Psychological Bulletin, 56*, 81–105.

9. Wright, H. F. (1967) *Recording and Analyzing Child Behavior*. New York: Harper and Row.

10. Lytton, H. (1971) Observation studies of parent-child interaction: A methods-logical review. *Child Development, 42*, 651–684.

11. Mitchell, S. K. (1977) The reliability, generalizability, and interobserver agreement of data collected in observational studies. *Dissertation Abstracts International, 37*(7-B), 3583.

12. Walsh, J., and Walsh, R. (1982) Behavioral evaluation of a state program of deinstitutionalization of the developmentally disabled. *Evaluation and Program Planning, 5*, 59–67.

13. Dawes, R. (1979) The robust beauty of improper linear models in decision making. *American Psychologist, 34*, 571–582.